Love & Support
in all
"WE" do
together!

Jerry Leonard
'2008

Many Hearts,
ONE SOUL

An American Perspective on the Work of Bert Hellinger

GARY STUART
EDITED BY GARY CORB

authorHOUSE™

1663 LIBERTY DRIVE, SUITE 200
BLOOMINGTON, INDIANA 47403
(800) 839-8640
WWW.AUTHORHOUSE.COM

First published by AuthorHouse 08/11/05

ISBN: 1-4208-7093-9 (sc)

Printed in the United States of America
Bloomington, Indiana

This book is printed on acid-free paper.

DEDICATION

To Bert Hellinger for developing this wondrous modality, to Margot Ridler for introducing me to it, to Heinz Stark for educating me in it, and to Gary Corb for helping me write about it. To all the aforementioned, and to all who read the following, I offer a sincere and humble "thank you."

NAMASTE,
GARY STUART

TABLE OF CONTENTS

PREFACE

*I*n the heart of the soul lies a great equanimity. Everything has its place; everything has its balance. There is even perfection in the counterbalance. However, we as a species seldom get the chance to reflect upon the existence of a natural order within all things -- the cosmos, our planet, even Man himself -- and it is with even greater infrequency that we get to witness how these elements affect the very existence of one another. In this work, I intend to present just such an overview, exploring the many diverse paradoxes of Divine intelligence at work within this "cosmic puzzle" of life. We will examine the wonder found in each individual piece, as well as the entire miraculous picture. But just as all the pieces of the puzzle coexist simultaneously, let us remain open to the great probability of life existing eternally with the past, present and future occupying this singular moment known as "now." This may seem a little far-fetched to some, but it is an important concept to grasp if we are going to attempt to analyze, and ultimately comprehend, the "big picture."

To present and examine this aforementioned macrocosm is admittedly a tall order, but life is too short for me not to do so. All I am offering is a personal peek into the profound epiphanies that seem to reveal themselves to me on a daily basis. Actually, this undertaking is hardly as presumptuous as it may appear. We all have access to that "inner ear." But who listens? Who processes? Who takes the time to share those thoughts and perceptions? We all share a commonality of profound awe living within this parameter known as life. The task of stopping and taking the time to report these observations is the obligation of the philosophers among us. Let me be the first to admit the enormity of this undertaking. Let me also state that my desire to do this comes from a place of unconditional love, fully and constantly aware of the Creator whose breath and vision I am going to attempt to interpret and communicate.

There is an intelligent, deep and profound simplicity to all things, despite their systematic complexities. Their subtle entwinements are often so awe-inspiring that we must stop in admiration at the wonder of it all. These discoveries are part of what I hope to share in the forthcoming pages. I hope to not only render palatable our modern day conundrums, but to inspire the mind to soar to those skinny branches of conscious awareness where the heart of the soul resides -- humbly, quietly and not so secretly.

Often our day-to-day struggles keep us so occupied with our little picture that we rarely have the time to pull back and consider the big one. Doing so, however, can be the real "pause that refreshes." For those to whom this idea appeals, this book is for you. For those who do not care about such contemplations, this book is also for you. Consider this your invitation to stop and ponder what you may be missing. Regardless of the levels of reality you are willing to admit exist, may this work inspire you to climb to new heights, explore new depths and contemplate the meaning of all things big and small. It is, after all, Man's awareness of his awareness that distinguishes him from most other life forms on Earth. This is his greatest blessing and greatest curse. It is this duality that seems to haunt our souls and makes us wrack our brains. It is the unconscious price we all pay for being conscious beings.

When I first discovered the work of Bert Hellinger, I was taken aback by the commonality of his observations and those of my own. He postulated the existence of a "family conscience," and of the hidden dynamics that influence how we react to various stimuli throughout our lives. He spoke of Man's ability to release himself from family patterns that do not serve him. He spoke of the Sacred existing in all things. Most intriguingly, he spoke of a love so unconditional and so inclusive that it could embrace all -- including hate. In other words, not only was he acknowledging those "bigger forces" at work, he had found a way for us to work with them. I knew I had to become a facilitator of this revolutionary process, which I have, and that someday I would be able to share what I had discovered during my years of practice, which I now do.

I believe we are entering an age of wholeness and unity for the body, mind and soul. The "dark age" of separation, ignorance and despair is coming to a close. The grand, unifying field is here, and it exists in the last place we would ever think to look -- inside our collective unconscious. Maybe humankind is capable after all of attaining the peace and grace that every other living thing seems to have mastered. Perhaps it is their lack of objectivity that gives them that illusive sense of grace, peace and harmony. Does a fly question whether it is a good day or a bad day? Does the cow question why the fly has chosen to land on him and judge whether that is good or bad? Does a plant question whether it should or should not grow a leaf because a caterpillar might eat it? Nature seems to inherently know its own soul as it lives in peace and goodness, flexibly changing with the wisp of a breeze or the lighting of an insect. There is a hidden conscious order contained within the seemingly chaotic randomness of life itself. In other words, the chaos is part of the order. But more on that later.

Please enjoy this love letter from my subconscious. These poems and essays are meant to help us all get to a place where we have a better understanding of "All That Is" and, above all, that all is good!

All is love or lack thereof!

In collective peace, harmony, prosperity and depth,
Gary Stuart

GENERATIONS

They gave
We receive
They die
We grieve
Life goes on, Life goes on

We give
They receive
We die
They grieve
Life goes on, Life goes on

The Beginning is the End as the End is the Beginning!

WE ARE OF THE EARTH

E arth itself has its own lifecycle -- grand, profound and simple all at the same time. To truly observe this cycle, we must suspend the belief that death is bad or that there actually is an ending to life at all. I believe, rather, that it is a transitory stage that all beings must go through in order to learn, suffer, grow and enjoy. It is our life experiences that enrich our journey, and they are as seasonal as winter, spring, summer and fall. Humans have the same life and death cycles as other life forms existing in nature -- the trees, for example. We all may appear to shrivel and die in our winters; but life, like energy, is never really extinguished. It merely changes form. We all stand here on the bones of our ancestors, looking at the same stars, breathing the same air. (Well, give or take a little photochemical smog.) We still look up in awe as they did to the noble redwood tree. The same wind that blew life into their beings now fills our every breath. Life is continually renewing itself. Nature has a way of maintaining order, even by means of events that appear chaotic. We must bear in mind that the Earth has its own lifecycle independent of Man. This is especially important to remember given the present concerns over the issue of "global warming." Our planet's climate will continue to fluctuate from cold to hot to cold, from dry to wet to dry, ad infinitum. Choose whichever order you like; one will always follow the other. The Cold Age can bring about a Hot Age, as the Wet Age can bring about a Dry Age, and vice-versa. It is part of the great Yin and Yang of life, and all life forms must learn to adapt to the ever-growing, ever-changing life force of our planet. Every plant, mineral and form of animal life, including Man, is part of this evolutionary process. This life force also resides in every cell of our being. To put it poetically, the stones are kin to our bones, the trees our lungs, the water our blood and the plants and animals our food. Everything is entwined in a great, intricate lattice of Divine creation. Even the often-vicious interactions between these elements help to maintain nature's delicate and perfect balance. Remember, the natural movement of all things is a positive one.

In times of turmoil, every life form will fight to the death for survival. Faced with the reality of receding water, a species will reduce its population to ensure the avoidance of extinction, thereby enhancing and strengthening the gene pool of the surviving members. Divinely "hardwired" into every species in existence is this hunger for life, this lust for survival. All will kill to live. After all, isn't Man himself a beast of the wild? Isn't civilization a righteous veneer to disguise our true heathen nature? On the African plain, a creature can perish as easily from a lack of water during a drought as it can at the jaws of a hungry predator at the local watering hole. Any lion worth its salt will gladly drink the warm, red blood that oozes from its freshly-killed meal. There is no judgment of good or bad associated with such an action. He is simply following his instincts and, in doing so, living in harmony with a Divine plan that may be bigger than the human mind can comprehend. These innate impulses may be bloodthirsty, but they serve as a strengthening, balancing mechanism for the animal population -- indeed, for all living things. This

3

"natural order" also pertains to the human species, as pointed out by Darwin many, many years ago in his "survival of the fittest" theory. Wild as it may seem, even human animals will kill or be killed in their quest to attain the resources necessary for survival. Even the "civilized" world of business becomes a jungle when Man follows his instincts. Every leveraged buyout or merger, every hostile corporate takeover, every pitting of one conglomerate against another finds root in the very same impulse felt at that shrinking watering hole on the African plain. Even in the wilds of the New York Stock Exchange, the strong are on the rampage and domination in order to survive is just business as usual.

The lion may be crafty in his own way, but human beings are able to employ more subtle dynamics to help ensure victory over their opponents. We can propagandize and create enemies of convenience. We can influence mass audiences through various media outlets. We can manipulate and mislead to elicit a desired response to a perceived threat. Human insecurities and personal paranoia, as history demonstrates, are often the facilitating factors that allow the dictators of the world to assume power. There will always be new enemies to pursue in the quest for that illusive feeling of safety. There are always new, even present-day aggressors lurking in the bushes. As primitive as the wildebeest is the belief that one can gain personal security by means of mass extermination. Such attempts reduced Jews of 1940s' Germany to thirsty antelope at a dwindling watering hole, and the Nazis to lions seeking dominance to survive. But let's not dismiss this metaphor as merely poetic; it has deep significance. There seems to be a strong, invisible link between the forces of life and the forces of death, between perpetrator and victim. Such relationships are evident in all human systems -- families, governments, nationalities, religions -- on every continent around the globe.

This remains as true for our time as for any. Indeed, it is almost as if we are engaged in a dualistic struggle of one consciousness verses another. It's fear and greed over love and abundance. It's the haves over the have-nots. First World dominance over the Third World doesn't denote a refined intellect. Whoever has the stronger army can overthrow a less-armed nation at any time for any reason or any whim. It may desire that country's resources, or claim it needs to provide protection from alleged threats, espousing the common good and promising safety for all concerned. Often, nations will unite and follow blindly, anxious to hate and wanting to kill those who are different. Although the victory and the spoils may initially go to the side with the most effective propaganda, the truth has a way of rising to the occasion and eventually shining victorious in the minds and hearts of the once-manipulated masses. Where regimes seek to create division, a sense of opposing unity often also becomes manifest. Empires rise and empires fall -- another law of Man's jungle. The cycle is never-ending; the Wheel of Life turns constantly and repetitiously, allowing us to discover what is new and rediscover what is not. The patterns we find in life are also found within our microcosm of life, our family system. Far from a solely private matter, these dynamics greatly influence our social and cultural interactions as well. We will examine these processes and explore their impact at length in later essays. For now, let it suffice to say that our planet's so-called "lower" life forms are not the only ones who struggle daily with the forces of life and death. Welcome to Earth in the 21st century. This is your world, too -- and you belong.

ONE 4 ALL 4 ONE

What is humanity's lesson at this point in time?

We are being taught and shown the "rules of life"
that apply to all living things,
yet we never stop to ponder the lesson unfolding right before
  our very eyes.
"ONENESS"

All existing in Nature are One with God.
Earth, Sky, Clouds, Trees, Land, Water, River, Lake, Ocean,
  Sea.
To pollute any is to pollute all.

All living things are One with God.
Sea mammals, Land mammals, Birds, Reptiles, Insects.

All of the unseen in the world are One with God.
Disease, Bacteria, Viruses, Atoms, Molecules, Elements.

All are part of the profound whole,
and God is the profound whole of all parts.
All living livings, all dying things, all are equal to the whole
and equally valuable as a part.

All aspects of life are inseparable from each other,
as life itself is inseparable from each part.

We indeed are one for all and all for one,
as the Creator's intention for us is to learn this truth
once and for all at this point in time.

L'Chaim!

EVERYTHING IS CONSCIOUSNESS!

*T*ruth be told, everything in the universe is energy. Each year, quantum physicists grow closer to discovering scientific proof of Einstein's Grand Unified Theory first proposed nearly a century ago. Stephen Hawking's "Brane" Theory and Columbia University professor Brian Greene's String Theory are further helping us to understand that, when it comes to the universe, the highest and lowest common denominator is consciousness.

Consciousness is manifest in all matter, dark or light.
Consciousness is manifest in water, polluted or clean.
Consciousness is manifest in the molecules of air, windy or still.
Consciousness is manifest in earth, lush or barren.
Consciousness is manifest in all living things.

Transformed, consciousness is even manifest in the death of all living things. Everything in the universe -- subatomic particles, migrating whales, orbiting electrons, orbiting planets -- is guided by a seemingly invisible, yet Divine, blueprint. With the utmost intelligence, it leads us in a never-ending cycle of birth and life and death, very much like the seasons of nature on Earth: spring, summer, fall and winter. Each phase lays the foundation for the next. But nature also has a way of throwing a few random elements such as free choice and chaos into the mix. This helps to keep the puzzle of life ever changing, and helps to keep us ever aware of its impermanence.

In observing nature at work, we can see that she possesses a profound intelligence -- a consciousness, if you will -- tantamount to revealing the mind of God at work. One could argue that, in her most nebulous state, God equals consciousness, which, in turn, equals the life force within all living things. Is this not the Divine plan that lies inside of each of us, guiding our every breath and every move as we feverishly swim in the enormous stream of life? Indeed, this seems to be humankind's biggest blessing and greatest curse: having the capability to observe ourselves both objectively and subjectively within this state of being -- aware of our awareness, as I like to say. Knowing who or what we think we are seems so very important to us, individually as well as collectively. Members of the human race seem to need some kind of security or certainty about their existence. It is as if we are on a very thin umbilical tether, wanting to be anchored in some tangible reality of our own making before we dissolve fearfully into thin air. No wonder religion has become such a powerful force within the human experience. We seem to have this inherent need to believe in something unknown, some tailor-made belief to help us trust in this earthly existence of ours. A spiritual understanding of our relationship with nature and with our Creator is one thing, but putting one's faith in the powerful, tax-free business of spiritual commerce can often lead to trouble. Those prone to greed and corruption have been known to dilute the message of salvation for their own ends. For millennia, the masses have been manipulated into adhering to so-called "sacred" religious edicts, often by means of the most profitable myth. "Organized religion," let's remember, is in the business of promoting "organized religion," not spirituality. Historically, disagreement gets one labeled a heretic -- punishable by death for even questioning The Myth. The fact that such decrees have been routinely imposed by those who claim to represent "God" is perhaps Mankind's greatest sin of all.

Human beings want so much to feel that they belong, that they are a real, solid and permanent fixture in what we call "physical reality." It seems as if, collectively, we are all scared little animals in this garden of earthly delights and do not trust ourselves to exist in this paradise without paying some kind of hefty price. The trauma imposed by the Adam and Eve fable goes on and on, and we continue to reap its bitter fruit -- GUILT. The only time we seem to allow ourselves a respite from this constant infighting with self-awareness is when we take our nightly excursion into the human brain's screensaver mode called sleep. Even in this naturally altered state, we often dream about whimsical events occurring as if we were still present in a physical reality. Does our consciousness ever rest? Are we always awake on some level? Are we always asleep on another? Doesn't our very existence provide a question to ponder? Read on.

CONSCIOUSNESS IS EVERYTHING

Consciousness is like an undulating amoebic cell -- energetically seeking awareness, intelligently pushing against its environmental boundaries, striving for life-affirming balance and fulfillment. Most of the time this constitutes a manifestation of goodness, but occasionally this balance is reestablished by means of destruction. All living beings are hardwired for survival and will attack, infect or kill a real or perceived threat at a moment's notice. The rules of life are pretty basic and simple: Kill or be killed; kill to eat; protect your young to the death. This is meant to insure the survival of each divinely unique genetic imprint made manifest by each conscious being. Arrogantly believing that these rules do not apply to us "civilized" humans is sheer folly. I may be oversimplifying things a bit, but if we are to understand what drives any conglomeration of living cells, we need to get down to the gooey, uncomfortable basics which apply to all multi-celled creatures known as living beings. The existence of any such being's "consciousness," however, is a matter of perception -- that of the quantum physicists verses the American Psychiatric Association.

One of nature's greatest motivators is hunger. Often, a creature's ability to survive is linked to its ability to kill. This can pertain to a being's hunger for sexual fulfillment, as well.

Some species develop visually stimulating plumage in order to gain another's fancy. Some will put up a valiant fight to win a desired mate. Many overcome seemingly insurmountable obstacles -- killing, willing to be killed just for the privilege of having sex. For the most part, most species just want to be left alone to eat and multiply in peace. Most want to rest up and sleep in safety before the next day's adrenaline rush kicks us into gear. Indeed, the Divine life cycle is pretty simple: **FORAGE, EAT, SLEEP, SHIT, FUCK, KILL, PARENT, DIE** -- in any order you choose. This may seem profanely oversimplified, but perhaps that's as it should be. After all, these impulses are at the core of every creature's being, and they (and we) embody both the sacred and the profane. When we study the neuro-chemistry of any animal, mammal, or even insect, we discover many striking commonalities. Even bacteria and assorted viruses have an innate desire to live and proliferate in a host environment that helps them to exist. In addition, all these life forms know, on some level, that they must instill certain lessons in survival into the consciousness of the next generation. Ironically, this information is often subconsciously communicated through various rituals within the familial system. A pack of elephants will gather to grieve the loss of one of their own. A flock of buzzards will begin to circle over their next easy meal. Every living thing knows what to do in any situation from either its natural instinct or its acquired intellect.

This leads us back to the subject of food. The desire for this most basic element of survival is more powerful than any weapon on Earth. Hunger can be used to manipulate or control anything or anyone. Just ask Mother, the provider of food in most homes throughout the world. Her decisions on the subject often override those of Father, the male breadwinner, as she feeds him along with the rest of the household. Though he may slave at a job he hates to provide the currency needed to buy the ingredients, he can often take second place or become invisible to his hungry brood chirping for their next meal. It seems this wondrous, undulating consciousness called hunger, which seeks fulfillment on a daily basis, is virtually a life force unto itself.

We will further address the hidden dynamics observed within family systems later in this book, along with the "order of love" as formulated by renowned author and lecturer Bert Hellinger. His amazing discoveries in the field of Systemic Family Constellation Work are some of the 20th century's most profound. After serving nearly twenty-five years as a Catholic priest -- two-thirds of that time as a missionary in South Africa -- Hellinger trained as a psychoanalyst in Vienna. However, other modalities such as Primal Therapy, Gestalt Therapy and Transactional Analysis seemed to offer a more experiential approach, and he began to develop his own integrative hybrid. Groundbreaking in its ability to access the unknown realms of the family's collective experience, the resulting process sheds new light on how family systems pass on certain "lessons" from generation to generation. Although communicated unconsciously, these lessons often weave a common familial thread. Perhaps Father never grieved the loss of his uncle; the familial lesson becomes, "Don't express grief." Perhaps Grandma had good reason to distrust Grandpa, but their granddaughter might just pick up on the message, "Don't trust men." Feelings of exclusion, insecurity, mistrust, unexpressed grief or anger -- these are all rather heavy burdens for our progeny to inherit, yet that's exactly what happens when such issues are allowed to retain their power within the family system. This is where the Hellinger work has proven most beneficial and effective. With the use of surrogates, the process can reveal the entire family system in microcosm, allowing the living consciousness of all generations, past and present, to give their messages of love and release so that each generation -- past, present and future -- may have a better life.

We are our ancestors' dreams come true!

When I first discovered Systemic Constellation Work, I found it to be so awe-inspiring, so deeply profound and "down-to-earth" simultaneously, that I knew I had to become a practitioner of such a magnificent modality. Indeed, after several years of extensive training, I received my certification from the prestigious Stark Institute in Germany and have been a working facilitator since 2003. Even after leading hundreds of workshops all around the United States, I still marvel at the ability of this process to reveal the pivotal dynamics that are often hidden within the familial system. Moreover, the effects of this work are quantum, benefiting not only the individual client, not only those within his or her family system, but all in attendance as well. Although we will discuss the "whys" and "wherefores" in subsequent essays, an overview of this modality should include a mention of this commonality, this communion of souls, if you will. Simply put, it is this "quantum" aspect of the process that allows it to work. By putting out the intent, by asking for help, we open ourselves to receive it.

Such energetic shifts fall within the facilitator's radar, as well. Although I've long been aware of my spiritual acumen, my involvement with this work has enabled me to understand even more about the role that unseen forces play in our day-to-day lives, as well as a deeper awareness of God/Spirit at large. These "bigger" forces subtly shape our daily existence within our sphere of life much the way gravity holds everything in its physical place. Such forces may not be seen, yet their effect is present in every move we make. It is reassuring, albeit admittedly surprising, that all is inherently good. Even pain is a valuable teacher. Many profound lessons are learned from seemingly negative experiences. With regard to the family system, there seems to exist an "ancestral field of awareness" which causes us to seek similar life experiences as a way of honoring the memory of those previous generations. Unfortunately, this often includes making similar mistakes and perpetuating a familial pattern of suffering. Such loyalty, while well intentioned, actually dishonors those ancestors by diluting the memory of what they endured. That was their hardship, their suffering. Repeating it doesn't help to end it. In fact, it merely ensures its continuation by relegating it to the next generation. Although these dramatic re-enactments are often done as a way of staying connected to the ones who came before us, I honestly believe that they would just as soon have their suffering pass away with them. The lighter our loads, the happier and more burden-free we are, the better we honor the legacy of those generations past.

Again, it is important to recognize the familial consequences of each generation's actions beyond the limit of that generation's lifetime. With this book, I hope to expose these consequences and, more significantly, reveal how to break their dysfunctional hold while still honoring the family system. I also intend to discuss Bert Hellinger's Trans-Generational work from a uniquely American point of view. In general, we in American society do not seem to acknowledge the importance of our ancestral connections as readily as, say, those in European societies, where Hellinger's work was developed. This is why, I believe, American families could benefit so greatly from this modality. Hence, this book. You might say I'm on a mission to get the Trans-Generational word out.

Audiences often ask me if I believe in "past lives." Although I do, family constellation work doesn't go there. I believe we need to get some clarity and understanding of this life before we go gallivanting into other dimensions. By building a solid foundation from the ground up, we begin to discover how everything fits into this grand, eternal experiment called life. In looking for the Divine in all things, we can see the subtle interconnections of our collective human experiences begin to reveal themselves. It is within this framework that we can explore not only our genetic family system (those whose DNA we hold near and dear) but also our national or cultural family (fellow Russians, Germans, Africans) as well as the family system from which we all emanate -- the human family.

Diversity + Unity = LIFE

Nothing is more complex and profoundly simple than that beautiful Spirit of Creation that guides all of life so eloquently, harmoniously and, yes, sometimes viciously. That God-like creator intelligence is always in control whether our diverse cultures are coexisting and finding unity within our common experiences on this blue celestial oasis or exhibiting those current and seemingly Cro-Magnon tendencies of touting war and death for the enrichment of the privileged few. Certainly, the ongoing commercialization of religion adds fuel to the hellfire, so to speak, by often encouraging such violent acquisitions in God's name. These proponents are not, as they claim, men of Spirit but, rather, men of "spear it and take it." One must wonder if our species is destined to live eternally in feudal times. After all, monarchs are still in power and pirates still plunder to achieve or maintain their CEO statuses. Sometimes it feels as if we are still just "cave dwellers" looking for safety and food, and that our age-old quest for survival is still all that really matters. Sometimes our minds are kept so busy with our daily chores that we forget to see the bigger forces at work within our lives. The magnificent garden is still alive and vibrantly diverse, despite the fact that we seem to be entering a spiritual Dry Age. We need to remember that we are all on the same journey -- a journey to unify our tender spirits with The One who has provided and created it all for our pleasure, amusement and occasional sorrow. Collectively and individually, the more we understand about what makes us tick, the more easily we can appreciate the great gifts we have inherited from our ancestors. In addition to the wondrous genetic information we all possess, perhaps there is another element of commonality The Ancient Ones have imparted. Perhaps, through our various life experiences, we are destined to understand how we all fit within this familial circle of the human race -- all living together as one on this finite planet, guided by a Divine intelligence we have yet to all recognize and which none of us can fully comprehend.

Therefore, from my loving heart to yours, I will attempt to share the vision with which I have been endowed and the gifts which I have received. Sometimes I feel as if I'm a harbinger, here to help my fellow human beings at this most critical point in our human history. I also recognize that this little calling of mine pales in comparison to all that is contained within, to anthropomorphize, the mind of God. I feel like a lonely neuronal cell just becoming conscious of the bigger, undulating brain into which we are all wired. I know that it's firing trillions of life or death impulses while busily balancing and creating a whole future of probable possibilities for the entire universe as we speak!

Still, I believe I'm up for the task. Let's go.

WE'RE ALL ONE

We are all ONE under the sun.
We are all ONE under this one sky.
We are all ONE of this Earth.
We are all ONE; this can never be undone.
We are all ONE and never have to question why.
We can all be ONE together and look to the sky.
Humanity as ONE will surely make us cry.

It is not believing this that makes many die.

We are all ONE in life and in death!

Being all ONE is a matter of breadth.

OUR SEXUAL DIVINITY

*T*his may be the best place to start, for it is at the very core of where we all began. Nearly every life form owes its existence to some form of sex. Certainly every animal and insect specie is perpetuated in this fashion. Even plants are part of a divinely interconnected ecosystem, although often unseen in this orgiastic manner. Unquestionably, we human beings have inherited an incredible gift in the form of our beautiful bodies, created from sexuality and designed to perpetuate sexuality. Every cell in our being recognizes the pleasure to be had from warm, wet friction culminating in a passionate, climactic release. Still, let's not dismiss this world-famous, hormonally-fueled desire as simply hedonistic. All forms of human sexuality also embody our highest and most divinely inspired acts of physical expression, those which unite us with another being for the purpose of mutual gratification or procreation -- or both. As mentioned earlier, making our unconscious desires conscious through physical action helps fulfill that inherent, divine need we feel to connect with one another. Not coincidentally, this could also plant the seed for a new being to come into existence to have its own turn at experiencing divine consciousness in its own new and unique way. Procreation is not, however, always the name of the game. Most of the time, sexual pleasure acts as the motivating factor, superseding reproductive duty. So often in family systems, it is discovered that an aunt or a grandmother, for example, was ostracized for indulging her sexual impulses outside the bond of matrimony. It wasn't that long ago that an unmarried girl would be forced into hiding by her family if she became pregnant. Messages of shame, guilt and embarrassment are easily passed down through a family system. Unconsciously, a granddaughter or niece will mirror the same "mistakes" as a way of keeping the alleged "black sheep" remembered and included in the family. Society has long sought to control sexuality by limiting its acceptability. Numerous religious organizations have sought to demonize our true human/animal nature. Yet, each generation continues to prove that sexuality is not controlled by a societal belief system and cannot be contained by imposing so-called "religious" dogma. Examples of sexual diversity are another unfortunate reason for familial exclusion. We must try to understand that all loving, sexual acts between any two of the same or of opposite genders are also valuable, as the expression in and of itself serves a higher purpose. Our natural impulses are something we all have in common whether we are strengthened by them, weakened by them or even become addicted to them. Regardless, we are all a little more human because of them. In fact, not only are our bodies designed for sex, but our minds, as well. Our brain is "hardwired" with ravenous hormonal instincts, and we are continually at its mercy. Neither will the innate power of our estrogen or testosterone be ignored. They are the carriers of that pulsating, Divine consciousness that seeks to make a connection, that seeks oneness and warmth, that seeks to manifest itself as a new being, a new experience. Is not the reproductive system itself a physical manifestation of the Creator in each of us? Although I wouldn't exactly say that God resides in our genitals, well… it's certainly a provocative and "pro-creative" notion.

While we experience consciousness in a variety of very real and physical ways, there are also many hidden dynamics which express themselves subconsciously through pleasure, love and desire. Such longings for physical self-expression course through our bodies as if we were puppets dangling helplessly, controlled by larger, biological forces. But, fear not. It is within these forces that, I believe, the wondrous and undulating energy known as Spirit resides. Wilhelm Reich called it "Orgone Energy." Modern science calls it the Big Bang with "dark matter." Could the mind of our creator consider reproduction to be trillions of "little bangs" with the energetic light of a spermatozoic comet fertilizing the dark singularity of a cosmic ovum? We can witness such processes quite magnificently through the wonders of time-lapse photography. Remember, we all burst forth out of an incredible orgiastic explosion of diverse and differentiated cells seeking unity and wholeness within the dark, warm, wet recesses of the divine feminine. As those cells, we sought and found completion, pleasure and life within the micro-universe of the uterus. **AND IT WAS GOOD!**

Considering that two unique halves make a perfect new whole, perhaps we should postulate "one plus one equals three." Maybe this is the true Holy Trinity. Perhaps that coveted Holy Grail is the birth canal -- the cup of the womb with two fallopian handles spilling forth a rich, dark, fertile wine. Man needs only add that missing ingredient by filling the chalice with a beautiful, pulsating, oozing phallus, thus unifying those diverse opposites that seek Divine unification. Perhaps the original sin was not the desirous influence of a woman, but Man's desire to leave Woman out of the Holy Trinity. Maybe there exists an undercurrent of belief that God is a feminine entity, hence woman's exclusion within the male dominated hierarchy of the church. Let us hail the

Divine Feminine. Let us admit that God He or God She is manifest in and from orgiastic pleasure. Let us create some healthy new principles of our shared sexual divinity. Down with sexual guilt and shame forevermore! Those judgments come from Man, not God. God is Life Force. God is our Biology. Sexuality is Good. Orgasm is Good. Orgasm is God. Reproduction is Good. God is Love. All Love is Permitted. Everything seeks Newness. Babies remind us to Love. Life goes On. All is Good!

All of life thrives on subtle and wonderful differences, so it follows that such differences would be found in sexuality, as well. Sexual diversity is an essential ingredient in nature's perfect system -- a safety mechanism as divinely inspired as heterosexual procreation. Homosexuality has been a part of the human experience since the dawn of human creation. To continue to demonize this natural inclination is to continue Man's attempt to demonize what he perceives as feminine, which only further encourages sexism. Remember, no homosexual was created from a same-sex union. All homosexuals are born and produced by heterosexuals, or at least by a combining of those certain male and female components. It is not a defect or disease as some so-called "bornagains" would have folks believe. With three billion potential couples and seven billion people in the world, there just might be a Divine method to diversity's alleged madness. Some people are called to serve our species in a different way. Humanity would never know the majesty of the Vatican's Sistine Chapel had Michelangelo a wife and kids to support. How ironic that "organized religion" expresses such condemnation for open and honest sexuality, yet will secretly practice what it preaches against. Then again, religion in and of itself seems to be continually prone to hypocrisy, be it sixteenth century Spain or twenty-first century America. The human race has overpopulated itself to the point of its own possible and self-created extinction. If nothing else, men loving men and women loving women could be viewed as a divinely inspired form of birth control. If we were created in God's own image, doesn't that go for everyone -- regardless of gender? Even if sexual activity is not involved, everyone has to gain from knowing intimately the many diverse aspects of love contained within the human heart. Sexual prejudice does a great disservice to our species, yet many continue to go through a vicious, almost paranoid state of rallying against what they do not understand. In a stroke of Divine irony, the Bible, by which they try to justify their bigotry, is actually about brotherhood and love for all mankind. Their very own savior never preached against homosexuality, yet they will selectively omit this fact from their allegedly Christian-conscious minds. Did Jesus ever desire to experience the divinity of a sexual union with another man? There are biblical references to his spending the night with a young boy in only sackcloth. And why were the apostles so misogynistic toward Mary Magdalene? Were they themselves jealous of her love for the Son of God? Again, for thousands of years, the church has been in charge of promoting... the church -- not the Spirit, not God. Claim as it might that they are synonymous, they are not. In light of the global AIDS pandemic, humankind has definitely proven that the church no longer has the power to subdue the pleasures of our human existence. The pandemic itself is a testament to the fact that people would rather follow their God-given instincts -- even if it means risking death -- than to live in the oppressive, guilt-ridden, hypocritical and dogmatic shadow of so-called "organized" religion.

SEXUALITY is GOOD
ALL are GOD & GOD is ALL

GOD IS A BABY!

God is a baby up in the sky.
If you could see him, you'd break down and cry,
then you would stop and start to ask why
do we hurt each other and make others die,
when God is a baby up in the sky?

God is a baby up in the sky,
smiling and laughing and understanding why.
We come here to learn; we come here to grow,
with souls that are pure as the white driven snow.

God is a baby so innocent so fresh.
She needs her own mommy to serve and protect
a soul that's so tender, so loving, so sweet.
Living as humans is so very complete.

God is a baby yearning to see
if he looks just like you or you look just like she,
as I look at you and I see
you look like me.

God is a baby; look at each other and see.
We are all baby gods yearning to see
that we're not here alone. Just open your eyes to see
that god is like you and you are like me.
Happy together is what we must be,
because God is a baby, and so now are we.

THE SACRED SYSTEM

*A*ll this talk of undulating consciousness and sexuality is merely an aperitif in preparation for this book's main course -- discussing the hidden dynamics in family systems as they pertain to Bert Hellinger's discoveries in the field of Systemic Constellation Work. As mentioned before, sexuality helps assure that life retains its cyclical and regenerative nature. Procreation, whether intentional or otherwise, exemplifies the power of our hormonally fueled desire for sexual gratification. It is yet another example of how that life force, that "undulating consciousness" will push the boundaries, so to speak, in its quest to perpetuate itself. In this modern age of AIDS, we bear witness to the fact that our species' ongoing need for sexual fulfillment is not easily quelled. The phallic fountain of life now sometimes begets death, yet cases of HIV and other STD's are at an all-time high. We have much to learn from this pandemic, and we will be discussing this again later on. Perhaps the undulating God consciousness seeks to know itself equally in life or death, with nothing lost and everything gained in either state.

There is no Destruction, only Transformation

Perhaps the life force itself wants to enjoy the unpredictable twists and turns as it experiences the duality of random chaos and inherent order. True life is never boring, as all existence is predicated on change. If consciousness has a goal, it just may be that of getting to know itself in every conceivable way. Consciousness finds growth within every challenge. It will push itself -- sometimes violently, sometimes peacefully -- down the cosmic stream, back to its source where its end and its beginning are one.

For the light of awareness to shine continually, everything must remain new, even though it may seem to stay the same. This newness must give birth to itself repeatedly, helping the present to become the past -- allowing life to begin anew. As a species, we build our families on the bones of our ancestors. They give us the support we need to assume the position of capstone on the pyramid of life. If nothing else, the knowledge of those generations past will be rediscovered, reinterpreted and re-experienced by the generation that now has its day in the sun. These life lessons could be exactly what the Shiva and Brahma (creator/destroyer) mean for us to learn. The Tibetan elders teach us that the Wheel of Life has to turn to find its fulfillment. Maybe it is the co-existence of life and death, victim and perpetrator, good and bad that helps to move life itself into the present moment -- and beyond. Not only does this duality propel us all into the unseen future, it supports us as we move forward toward our inevitable demise, which ultimately serves to fuel an inevitable rebirth.

THREE SECRETS

All that grows will die and dying nourishes what lives.
Life begets death as death begets life.
The secret of life is death and the secret of death is life!

Now where is this more evident within the human experience than in the creation of the next generation? From something as small as a microscopic yet passionately driven sperm and a receptively divine egg comes something bigger than the two elements themselves -- a new life, smaller than its creators, yet also bigger. From the undulating climactic union of two people uniting in orgiastic pleasure, a new vessel is created to experience life's perpetual newness, and to bestow that feeling of newness on the entire family system. Life passes through their loins and, in the process, transforms everything in its path. The couple becomes parents, the baby becomes a child and a unique, new branch joining two family trees is formed.

1 + 1 = 3

Nature is not one to sit back, however, and rest on her laurels. Even though there is now a new little life in the world, nature's job is far from finished. Not only are changes continually taking place within the baby's own body, but it is also creating new adjustments for the parents who now must learn to cope with the ever-changing needs of their little progeny. In a way, childbirth steals the title of "the younger generation" away from the parents and gives it to the infant. But before you're tempted to blurt out a dismissive "well, duh," let me just add that it is extremely important to understand this significance if we are to understand the ramifications of trans-generational issues. Children need to be protected. Children need to be nurtured. When people become parents, thus suddenly becoming members of the "older generation," they are faced with the task of fulfilling these needs, even if they never got those needs met themselves. Remember, childbirth creates not only children, but parents as well. As such, the parents who are thus created can no longer merely be their parents' children. The trans-generational effect is now in play. In other words, the entire dynamic of the family is changed. As the couple is transformed into parents, their own parents' roles shift into that of grandparents. Brothers and sisters suddenly become uncles and aunts. By simply existing in the world, one little newborn forever changes it. Life lessons become more substantial. Priorities become re-evaluated. Everyone involved is exposed to the wonderment and awe of how life itself is bigger than all its inhabitants put together, yet small as that swaddled innocent passed from chest to chest as it is kissed, hugged, nurtured and loved by all. Most predominately, however, we see the power of motherhood, the divine feminine, in all her glory. She comforts us. She protects us. She makes us feel good. She makes us feel safe. She nurtures us until we feel strong enough to leave her divine breast and wander out into the world, traditionally the father's "domain." (I mean that archetypically, not chauvinistically.)

As I mentioned earlier, we are the capstone of our family's generational pyramid. They help to support us; they help us to stand tall, even though we may not always be aware of it. No matter what we think of them or what we believe or even how we feel, **we belong**. Each successive generation has its own way of coping and dealing with what life has to offer -- and often what life has to offer includes death. Indeed, somewhere during the span of every lifetime, all living beings are forced to face this most difficult circumstance. Without question, one of the most painful and tragic types of death with which to deal is that of a child. Such an event often creates more grief because of the seeming injustice of life itself to take one so very young. Most human beings would rather avoid, deny or ignore the emotional pain that death has to offer. Adding tragedy atop tragedy, such decisions create a prismatic generational effect within the family system -- a life lesson of sorts on how to avoid or deny the pain rather than going through the process of releasing the grief. Without such a resolution, the weight of the unfinished event remains within the family, passed down the generational line as a dysfunctional coping mechanism. What could have been a catalyst for support at a time of loss, instead, becomes a lifelong, internalized burden. The reasons for and examples of such denial are as individual and diverse as the circumstances surrounding the death itself. In addition, the behavioral information inherited by the future generations serves not only as a template for how to repeat the pattern of avoidance, but the pattern of tragedy as well. All too often an all-too-familiar scenario will replay itself within a family system -- a fatal accident, a chronic disease, a murder. It is as if there exists a "family mindset" that agrees to create a shared experience of trauma within the lineage -- a generational self-fulfilling prophecy, if you will. For instance, the father of a young woman may have committed suicide many years ago. Instead of embracing the grief and, thereby, allowing herself to release it, she has kept it inside and allowed it to mutate into anger. Not surprisingly, her own son now exhibits similar feelings of frustration. He feels the loss as well, having never known his grandfather aside from what he has heard his mother say, perhaps in anger. Remember, the family system wants to be whole; it wants to be inclusive. Therefore, in an ironic attempt to include and have a connection with his missing grandfather, the son may actually attempt to create a similar fate for himself. Unconsciously, his actions would also serve as a karmic reminder to his mother about the grief with which she had not yet dealt -- yet with which she is all too familiar.

Familial patterns of tragedy and loss are an obvious example of how a family system replays its scenarios. Often, however, the patterns are more subtle. For instance, a woman, now a grandmother, may have had a stillborn child many years ago. Grief-stricken, she may have blamed the husband or father for creating the condition of the pregnancy in the first place, rather than allowing herself to feel the depth of the tremendous loss. "It was his fault this happened to me!" "I'm never going to let him or any man touch me again!" Instead of facing and working through the sadness, she chooses to fill the perceived emptiness in her heart with anger -- an anger that stays within the family system. Decades later, the unspoken generational lesson for her granddaughter could be "Don't trust men" or "It's their fault," hence giving the subliminal message, "You should blame ALL men for every pain that life gives you." Although prejudicial programming concerning the opposite sex does, of course, work both ways, I have been amazed to discover just how prevalent such "female-concerning-male" admonishments are within a great many family systems. Such unconscious programming actually serves to discourage us from feeling and resolving the negative aspects of events as they occur. Future generations of women born into such systems may retain that "do not trust men" message subconsciously, and look for men to provide the evidence to prove that philosophy (and great grandmother) correct. Perhaps a similar event, such as a pregnancy, could cause a similar feeling to manifest -- especially if one were carrying the great grandchild of the ancestor who had had the stillborn, for example. Make no mistake, unless certain disserviceable patterns are acknowledged and consciously altered, all subsequent generations will inherit the issues and behaviors of their forebears regardless of whether they knew them or not. In my practice, I often see clients who are continuing to feel the adverse effects of unresolved issues that are in excess of 100 years old. It is almost as if the energetic entanglements of our ancestors live on in our subconscious. We may not always feel those energies lurking there, but if the right event should rattle our ancestral framework, more than not, our reaction will be identical to those who came before us. In other words, I believe we inherit a lot more than DNA from our ancestral family line. In experiencing the profound work of Bert Hellinger, I have discovered the ways in which we can access these covert realms and, through the systemic constellation process, complete the unfinished business so that it need not remain ours. When we can objectively view the burdens we are carrying, we are empowered to make different choices and create healthier patterns in our own lives rather than, by rote, repeating ancestral behaviors that yield the same non-beneficial results.

Ultimately, life is ours to enjoy. Life is good. Everything that happens is good. Life is about learning how to be flexible, how to travel in its undulating flow. The journey can be rocky at times, challenging us with turbulence and difficult choices. At other times, the ride can be blissfully smooth. Still, life strives to succeed, to replicate itself and to continue its journey into infinity -- or at least beyond what we sometimes call "death."

Personally, I believe life can teach us the most at the most seemingly inopportune moments. The old adage, "When life deals you lemons, make lemonade," really is a valuable one to bear in mind, especially when you feel like you're up to your you-know-what in the stuff. Remember, some of our most important life lessons we learn from our worst experiences. From a trans-generational perspective, even a family's dysfunction is handed down with love and care. It is not our place to judge our family systems as "good" or "bad." They led to our creation and should be honored and respected, as we should honor and respect the gift of life they gave to us. Even in cases of emotional or physical abuse, there is an attempt being made to share a systemic experience. While this, in no way, rationalizes or excuses such ill-treatment, it serves as yet another all-too-common example of how strong our connections are to the behaviors of our parents and grandparents. Indeed, sometimes it seems as if we arrive with our homework all done for us, and it is simply our job to see how our forefathers arrived at those answers. We may often feel as if it is our legacy to recreate the patterns handed down as a symbolic way of showing respect. *"You suffered in this way and so shall I, as we are of the same blood, and this is the least I could do to show you I belong."* In truth, we have always belonged; we just thought we had to earn the privilege rather than simply being deserving of it. Hellinger finds that the gift of life itself is so great that the child may feel that he or she, out of guilt and great love, has to pay for the right to exist. The child may, in a desire to help his or her creators, unconsciously agree to take on familial pain, hold unpleasant memories, begin to express (or suppress) anger, or carry someone else's guilt. When a child isn't allowed to be a child, he or she becomes a parent to the parents, and the entire systemic family order becomes jumbled. Dysfunction then takes root to compensate for the disruption in what Hellinger calls "the order of love." Such dysfunction may serve as a quick fix to help ensure the family system's survival, but at what cost?

Again, sometimes it seems as if we are slaves to our "gut reactions." When confronted with stressful situations or difficult decisions to make, we very often defer to some predetermined inclination instead of recognizing that we have a conscious choice. Systemically, we seem to seek the same stimuli as was encountered by those who came before us so that we can have the same responses as those who came before us. Maybe human beings simply like certainty. Maybe it's simply easier to be a follower than a leader. Maybe the range of human emotion and behavioral choices is much narrower than one would think. Subconsciously, we all know that the time we have to inhabit this physical realm is extremely short. Perhaps we are all simply looking for some continuity.

As similar as we all are, however, I believe that each individual has an important and unique perspective to bring to humanity's table. I believe we can change our perceptions of and reactions to life's challenges, and that we are not merely trapped inside a timeless, holographic, generational prism. Simply put, I believe we can retain our continuity with those previous generations without bringing their "baggage" with us into the future. In fact, this is precisely what the Trans-Generational Constellation process allows us to do. Through this extraordinary modality, we can see just how our perceptions of our earthly experiences have been framed and structured for us by our family's energetic imprinting. Imagine being able to find, frozen in time, the origin of an infamous, irksome or even detrimental ongoing family dynamic. This work gives us a second chance, so to speak -- a chance to witness the true emotional underpinnings of the issue and to look objectively at the situation without any judgment and with total equanimity. From this perspective, we are able to see how the family system began to hold on to the energy rather than releasing it or bringing it to some resolution in its proper historical context. Perhaps grandfather never said, "I'm sorry." Maybe grandmother never said, "Good-bye." This work gives us the chance to change the energetic pattern of the family system. While the acceptance and subsequent release of the old patterns may prove to be one of the most liberating experiences one could ever imagine, the road to such enlightenment may not always lead where expected. The energies that manifest within the confines of the constellation may not always reveal what the ego might prefer. Remember, in order for an old pattern to be broken, an energetic shift must take place -- and a shift in perception is a great place to start. The information revealed may not initially reflect the story that the conscious mind thinks it knows; however, when the truth is finally discovered and given a voice, we can feel the energetic shift within our very bones. By accepting and embracing these truths, we give ourselves new and different options rather than simply choosing the well-worn, systemic, dysfunctional ones that we seem to select out of habit rather than choice.

As the saying goes, "Everything is love or lack thereof." Knowing our family's original "order of love" can help us navigate the path back to a wholeness that we might not have even consciously known was missing. The energy of our consciousness wants to "get it right," so to speak -- wants to learn something new, wants to experience profound joy. As a species, humanity still seems to be in its infancy in many ways. Human beings achieve true adulthood by learning to take personal responsibility for their actions and for any consequences arising from those choices. In doing so, we free ourselves from the shackles of the past and break those dysfunctional, trans-generational patterns of victimization. Believe me, a little honor and respect can work wonders. By re-establishing the system's true order, we give ourselves the opportunity to create something exciting and new. Who knows? Perhaps it could be inner peace, personal power, wisdom, maturity, even a more functional adulthood. What a concept!

GRIEF

Grief oh grief
You're like a lowly thief in the dark of the night
As you cut a deep wound as sharp as a knife

Grief oh grief
You stole my loved one and took their life
Now all I feel is an endless strife

Grief oh grief
You can never be denied
Because all you do is make people cry

Grief oh grief
You are so crafty and sly
and act as insidious as a dangerous spy

Grief oh grief
Why do you leave us in the dark
as you steal a body and leave your mark?

Grief oh grief
You mercilessly feed on life's fragile "spark"
and leave us great sadness that's locked in our hearts

Grief oh grief
We must let you go to prove to ourselves
that we are in control

Grief oh grief
You haven't conquered my soul.
I'm taking charge now and letting you go!

GENERATIONAL FAMILY ORDER

*E*ach generation's story continues that of all the previous. Each living thing gets its day in the sun. What seems most fascinating to me is that the lessons and issues with which our ancestors dealt did not simply die along with their bodies. The experiential fallout, if you will, is passed on to the successive generations whether they knew their relatives or not. "Systemic Family Constellation Work," the process coined and developed by Bert Hellinger, explores just how the family system came to be established many, many generations ago. Each system contains its own self-perpetuating life force possessing all of the family's historical information -- its lessons and traumas, positive and negative -- as if it were contained inside the genetic code itself. Part of what makes the Hellinger work so profound has been the discovery of those clandestine elements that, while energetic in nature, become realized as conscious dynamics within the system. They are much like their macrocosmic counterparts, those invisible gravitational forces that hold the sun, planets and moons of our solar system together while balancing elliptically around yet another system, the Milky Way, which, in turn, has its own galactic orbit, as well -- gyroscopes within gyroscopes, if you will. Astronomically or biologically, it all may seem random and chaotic; yet there is an order to its flow, and it all fits seamlessly and exists in perfect harmony. There are certain rules of consciousness hidden within our family systems, however, that need to be recognized in order for such familial harmony to occur. For this to be achieved, both within the system and within ourselves, we must remain mindful of our family's correct "order of love," as Mr. Hellinger has so elegantly coined it. As simplistic as it may sound, we need to acknowledge, honor and respect all of our ancestors, including our parents and older siblings. I know this is easier said than done, yet it is important to do so. By showing them respect, we show respect to the proper hierarchical order of the family system. It is out of balance for the newest branch of the family tree to judge and criticize the other branches or its trunk. Truly, how could anything about this tree be "bad?" It gave you life. It even gave you the ability to grow your own tree.

In the animal kingdom, a family system is typically started when a male chooses a female to bear his children. So it is among human animals, as well. When a man and woman unite and have a child, that child becomes the newest member of that family system. Of course, that baby looks up to its parents, inherently trusting them and reaching out to love them unconditionally, smiling on his or her creators in adoration as if to say, "Good job, Mommy! Good job, Daddy!" When other siblings come along, the oldest child still takes precedence over the younger ones just as the parents still take precedence over the child and the grandparents still take precedence over the parents, and so on and so forth. Symbolically, if not literally, that baby looks up to two parents with four grandparents behind them and eight great grandparents behind them and sixteen great, great grandparents behind them and… well, you get the idea. There is great power and wisdom to be gleaned from each one of their lives -- each one of their hearts waiting to share with that new little life who had the power to shift their generational roles. Theirs is a great force of experience and stability, ever-present in its support of the forthcoming generations. Again, the family system is a pyramidal one, and we are the current capstone. Those previous generations provide the strength and confidence that supports us until we start a pyramid of our own -- and thereby become part of the foundation. Even less-archetypal families, such as lesbian or gay male couples, still have a divine order and are still very much included as part of a system. I have simply been using the heterosexual relationship as a family model. As most of us know, there are also valid families with parents of the same gender, and they share a similar "order of love," be it two men, two women, or a "trans-gendered" household. Though it might appear more complicated on the outside, there is still a family system at work, and most of the inner, hierarchal "orders" still apply. Remember, a majority of all human beings have been created through heterosexual encounters. No one has incubated for nine months in a test tube just yet. There are, however, rare cases where a woman's mother has acted as a gestational surrogate for her, thereby bearing her own grandchildren. By in large, though, our discussion of this work will focus on the norm -- with some slight variations on the theme.

Anyone born into any family system, which is everyone, has a place. We also have an opportunity to expand that role as life presents its unexpected challenges and unpredictable twists of fate. The bottom line is that everybody belongs, even if they think that they do not. There is an invisible, genetic bond that can never be broken. This is equally true for those of us who were adopted into a family system outside of our biological one. Such cases, understandably, generate many unique dynamics that we will be discussing at length later in this book. Regardless of circumstance, however, every being in every system has a right to express and celebrate his or her special purpose, in all its glory or horror, throughout his or her entire lifetime. Ideally, the structure of the family should work to support and even encourage such individuality. In reality, many family systems unconsciously work to exclude such "black sheep." Still, Hellinger observes that such a dynamic might also be viewed as "ideal" since it has contributed to that family member's existence and, therefore, should not be judged as anything but ultimately good. For those of us who may feel excluded from our family's system, that bond that might seem non-existent is, in reality, stronger than we would ever allow ourselves to believe. If there is one thing I've learned from my years of doing this work, it's to never say, "I'm nothing like my mother!" Falser words were never spoken, and fate will work overtime to prove them wrong. Although, in most cases, it is the man who starts the family system (hence our family surname), it is the bond between mother and child, whether she is married to the father or not, that is the strongest of all. Yet, despite the father's being outside of this intimate, cellular bond, both partners are essential for the process to happen. In other words, men are as important as women and vice versa. People are inherently equal, despite having different roles. In many cases, the father traditionally provides the safe little nest for the family and the means to feed his wife and children. From the child's point of view, however, these contributions may not even be noticed, much less appreciated. In fact, such a father could be seen as "absent" since, not being at home, he would often miss out on the day-to-day developments for which the mother would be present. After months and months in utero, followed by years and years in childhood, this mother/child bond is undeniably one of the closest and often most covertly influential we will ever encounter.

There is also a strong bond we feel to the culture that helped to support our ancestral beginnings. This link with our "mother country," if you will, as well as the history behind the events that affected our ancestors there, often has more of a profound impact on our sensibilities than we are willing to admit. Even if those ancestors had to leave their homeland, emigrating to freedom or fleeing to save their lives, the familial connection to our country of origin remains a powerful one and needs to be acknowledged by the family's subsequent generations. It is also important to remember that life goes on despite the turbulence in and misfortunes of this seemingly less-than-perfect world. When we allow ourselves to remain flexible enough to roll with the punches, we somehow become wise enough to see that, even at its most tragic, life is inherently good. Granted, it may be hard at times to find that proverbial silver lining, but have faith -- it is there nonetheless; we need only to recognize it. Human beings, remember, have survived all manner of chaotic ups and downs. Perhaps it is our connections, both seen and otherwise, that provide us the stability to steer through life's roughest seas. After all, we have inherited an effervescent and wondrous consciousness from our effervescent and wondrous Creator. The life force that is behind the true system is very forgiving and, actually, very pliable -- able to adjust to the unexpected yet internalized forces of trauma, tragedy and horror, as well as the day-to-day ones involving relationship issues such as divorce or adoption. Indeed, "the Devil is in the details," so to speak.

In every family system, there exists an energetic field of familial beliefs that Hellinger refers to as "the knowing field." These conscious and unconscious beliefs and strategies seem to be holographically entwined, combining the current family system with all the other systems that came before -- those of the parents, grandparents and great grandparents -- from both sides of each ancestral line. In other words, it is as if everyone who has ever existed in our family's system is living within our DNA, or at least stored within our subconscious, feeding us our innate impulses as we go through life. This encoded information also plays a pivotal role in establishing our cultural tone, as well as influencing our reactions to others. Generally speaking, when the order of the system is respected, health, inner peace and harmony have a chance to follow. As life would have it, however, there are always plenty of unexpected variables thrown into the equation to help keep us alert, alive, awake and aware. That old applecart can be upset in any number of ways -- financial challenges, heartache, disease, miscommunication, family tragedy -- a whole gambit of seemingly random and potentially terrible circumstances. Sometimes the family is the victim of such negative events. Sometimes it's the perpetrator. Yet, every family system has a way of regaining its stability, often counterbalancing negative experiences with positive ones to help ensure its ultimate survival. It is as if each player in the system knows his or her job and what must be done in order to maintain the systemic equilibrium, both on an individual and a collective level. Shakespeare's observation, "All the world's a stage" may indeed be right. We are but mere players in this piece called life -- pawns on a chessboard, to mix metaphors. We owe our strategy to a greater game master, a higher force that has a direct effect on our responses to life's stimuli. With regard to the family system, each agrees, though perhaps not consciously, to pay the price or suffer the consequences for any injustices incurred by any member of that system. Each family has a history that follows it like the tail of a comet, pushing into the unknown, lighting its way into eternity. Without the comet, however, the tail would cease to exist.

Ideally, a family system can provide the best of all possible worlds. We can receive encouragement. We can learn compassion. We can even feel loved and supported. Furthermore, each successive generation has the opportunity to strengthen its ties to the group. Yet, being a member of such a system can sometimes involve the worst of all possible worlds. Sometimes we are tested to see just how we cope with those curve balls that life tends to throw our way. Although one of the most common, the death of a family member is also one of the most traumatic experiences we will ever have to face in our lifetime. Regardless of the circumstances, it is always difficult to navigate that temporary river of sorrow when one of our own appears to have been lost into an unknown sea. Still, it is our response to such an event that determines whether our ties to the family system become strengthened or weakened as a result. Often our uneasiness lies in our selfishly seeing the reflection of our own mortality -- an awkward awareness that our state of being could be snuffed out at a moment's notice. In the bigger picture, however, perhaps we should be secretly grateful that there are no guarantees in this miracle called life. Although it may be hard to make sense of any such situation, the grief of a parent who loses a child is undoubtedly one of the most difficult to bear. In his work, Hellinger has found that even miscarriages and abortions must be grieved and included in the family system if any semblance of peace is to be attained. Without such familial inclusion, it is as if an energetic black cloud is hovering within the system, remaining for generations beyond the event itself. Only when the child's rightful place within the family is recognized can a feeling of true harmony be restored. Other times, it may be the premature death of a parent that wields a devastating blow. When a child is forced to grow up quickly, meaning he or she takes on the role of a parent, the entire family system is adversely affected because the "order of love" becomes confused. When someone isn't really allowed to be a child, it's often difficult for him or her to relinquish control and share responsibility as an adult. The Trans-Generational Constellation process affords us the opportunity to re-establish the correct familial order and allows an adult of any age the much-needed chance to feel like a little, innocent child again -- perhaps even for the first time.

Indeed, loss and grief seem to be the most crippling of emotions to the human race. Maybe the notion that this is all a temporary state discombobulates us. Maybe our fear of impermanence stops us from really connecting to life and the love it has to offer. Maybe the distance we keep in order to buffer the pain we feel when a loss occurs also numbs us from the joys we could be feeling as well. As Helen Keller once wrote, "There is no security; life is a grand adventure or nothing!" Even if our physical body is only a temporary gift, we would each do well to appreciate that spark of life that resides within it. Those who would go so far as to disregard that spark by taking away another's right to exist will not only bear a heavy burden within their own soul but within the heart of their entire family system, as well. Looking at the "big picture," who's to say if the fate of both the killer and the victim perhaps had an unfathomable date with destiny? It is not our place, therefore, to judge those bigger forces that may have chosen them to act out a personal, political or national drama. We must simply agree that it is so. It is done, and somewhere in the craziness of all that is meant to be, it was good. It is actually just as destructive to hold onto remorse and feelings of hatred for the perpetrator as was the murderous act itself. Remember, such anger gets passed down the generational line. Children and grandchildren often spend their lives fighting battles for ancestors they never knew. More importantly, those battles were their ancestors', not theirs. One of Hellinger's most intriguing observations is that the energy of a killer or perpetrator becomes part of his or her victim's family system. This is, in part, why there can be no peace on either side until the victim and the perpetrator are able to reunite. Admitting that it was the fate of both family systems unifies us to that higher consciousness and, thereby, serves the greater good. This new attitude is especially important in helping the surviving family members to release the pain of the past and move forward into a better and more functional future. This, of course, is the entire point of the Trans-Generational Constellation process, and I will discuss more about just how such resolutions are achieved in later chapters.

Thank God, literally, that people who have had NDE's (near death experiences) report that it's an exhilarating journey back to the compassionate, white, loving light of the Source where all is understood and all is forgiven. It is comforting to know that, on the other side of the looking glass, we will all be reminded of just how loved we really are. God probably shakes her head in disbelief that we give each other -- and ourselves -- such a hard time. From our Earth-bound perspective, of course, it is a very different story. At times, our existence seems a study in duality as we valiantly try to make that lemonade out of life's plentiful lemons. Again, it's hard to see the big picture when we're trapped inside our little dramas. Of course, I do not mean to be frivolous about the tragedies and traumas with which we must all cope at one time or another. From a child's perspective, for instance, the loss of a parent may appear to be an insurmountable obstacle. Naturally, such grief can be tremendous for anyone at any age, but for children it can be especially confusing. Should the mother or father choose to remarry, the child will likely go through a period of feeling that insult has been added to injury. Though they may often deny it, children have a deep and everlasting loyalty to those whose gene pool they share. In other words, the child's sense of loyalty to his or her deceased parent may become challenged when the surviving parent's new spouse enters the picture. This new member of the system may pick up on the strained dynamic and feel the frustration of being compared to and having to compete with someone who's dead. The child, of course, may feel no loyalty nor show any respect to the new stepmother or stepfather. Furthermore, the new spouse may grow to resent being "stuck" with someone else's children. You see how quickly the family system's dynamics can become convoluted? In addition, these layers of hidden energies and subtle resentments actually get stuck within the system. Ironically, when the child leaves home to start his own system, he will most likely vow never to make the same mistakes nor force his child to endure the same painful situation as he did when he was a boy. Of course, this all but ensures that the pattern will continue. As the saying goes, "What we resist persists." Until the negative energy is acknowledged and released from the system, it simply gets passed on to the next generation to deal with. That generation then feels the pressure of having to finish old business in addition to playing whatever hand life has dealt them. Mind you, this passing on of ancestral baggage is done unconsciously and with an ironic undercurrent of intended service to the family system. What differentiates the Hellinger approach from other modalities is the acknowledgment that, at our deepest level, we do it all gladly and with love. Without even intending to, we carry a mantle for the system that gave us the gift of life. In doing this work, I've discovered that the weight of the issues that I carried for my parents was actually much bigger than the pain or the trauma I thought I had to endure. In other words, I wasn't so much carrying those familial traumas; I was carrying the

WEIGHT of those traumas. This is precisely how the energy of our ancestors' life experiences remains very much alive within our family systems. In my case, I had subconsciously picked up the nonverbal cues and had carried them on top of my own perceived childhood traumas. I was further amazed to discover the depth of the pain I chose to shoulder. The biggest surprise, however, was that I loved those people so deeply that I would agree to let myself be hurt if it would somehow serve the greater family system. I was speechless and shocked to discover the depth of my love for those very people I thought I hated. I was exposed to the raw truth that I loved them with all of my heart and would do anything, including self-sacrifice, to belong. Of course, this is one of the many paradoxes we uncover in doing Trans-Generational work. Letting ourselves be victimized does not serve the family system. Repeating dysfunctional patterns of behavior only serves to perpetuate dysfunction. We cannot carry someone else's pain for them. More specifically, we do not have to try.

Systemic constellation work allows us to release ourselves from those negative energetic patterns and, at the same time, helps transform them into a surprising source of support from those who suffered before us. Again, there are many ways in which people deal with grief and the loss of a loved one. Attempts at denial concerning the death often bring about some rather bizarre and detrimental behaviors. Some will become sick with the same fatal disease, perhaps showing a karmic solidarity with the deceased family member. Another may have a similar accident or subconsciously put himself in similar danger or at similar risk. Others may simply drink their sorrows away or take drugs to avoid the unpleasantness of death. Still others may take their own lives outright as payment of a perceived family penance. In other cases, some try to take the place of a lost parent by stepping into that role in order to help the family system left behind. My own father died at a relatively young age from malignant throat cancer. Being the only male child, I tried to take his place by being a junior dad to my six younger siblings as well as a companion to my widowed mother. I was only sixteen at the time and, having been a battered child, thought I would never miss or need to grieve a man I thought I didn't love. Subconsciously, I wanted to help my broken family system to remain whole, regardless of any personal cost. As an adult, I have come to learn that my unique childhood situation really wasn't all that unique at all. Family systems have an agenda of sorts -- to survive, succeed and live on past any trauma or through any drama. Various family members, however, may exhibit a variety of reactions as diverse as the events themselves. Some may run away to escape something that can't be undone. Others may become depressed at the perceived hopelessness of the situation. Still others express their grief as anger or frustration and may begin to distrust other loved ones. Indeed, the same external stimuli can trigger a myriad of varied internal responses. These responses, then, become part of the family legacy, and their example often establishes a systemic behavioral pattern.

Where Bert Hellinger has excelled is in being able to help us see the unseen, feel the unknown, resolve the irresolvable and, most surprisingly, actually feel good doing it. It is within his Family Constellation process that such revelations occur. By looking beyond our conscious beliefs, we are able to access the core energy behind those beliefs which is fueling our current behaviors, thereby allowing us to resolve an issue at its roots. In doing this, we acquire a remarkable objectivity as we experience and begin to internalize the bigger, often archetypal truths regarding our eternal family system. Such an epiphany transcends space and time. It is a moment of quantum proportions where the past, the present and a new and probable future merge. Here, we are allowed a glimpse of whatever came before us, manifest in all its dynamic glory or horror. We can facilitate and witness the completion of any and all unresolved issues that continue to haunt the family system generation after generation. It is truly awe-inspiring to watch how the familial stories we thought were etched in stone begin to break apart and crumble, along with our preconceptions and beliefs about those stories and their characters. As a result, a new understanding emerges -- a deeper compassion, a previously unknown strength -- as we watch our family system's "back story" rewrite itself right before our eyes and ears. You are hereby invited and encouraged to suspend your disbelief. While I know this process may be difficult to comprehend, trust me, once you've experienced it, the revelations and resolutions will astound you. The energetic truth, so to speak, shall set you free. There's hope. There's a way out. There's an end to the suffering incurred from those unresolved issues of generations gone by.

Sometimes the only way out is through!

LOVE LETTER

Dear Father,

From your loins I sprang forth into the infinite possibility of life as I entered the home of my gestation, my mother's womb. I am forever in your debt.

Dear Mother,

From your womb I was nurtured and grew into the person I was yet to become, the progeny you risked life and limb to create. I will remain forever in your debt.

Dearest Parents,

I will always remain small and humble to the fact that I am a joint creation of you both and forever remain proof of the union of your passion and love in that spectacular moment of conception as you both became **one** in orgiastic pleasure, two humans seeking divine completion through sexual pleasure. I am the product of the oneness you desired. I am the one that proves to you that that moment in time was sacred and can never be undone, as I am your humble child forevermore.

I want to learn everything about you both. I want to help in any way I can. I will do anything to keep that loving moment alive between you both. I will pay any price you ask, for my devotion to you knows no limits. I will gladly sacrifice all I have to honor you *both, as you are my creators who blessed me with this body and this life. I know it can never be repaid but I'll try to do good, be helpful and reflect the wonder back to you that you both endowed me with as your child. Thank you both for this opportunity to live and experience all life has to offer. Thank you both for this opportunity to give. Thank you both for the chance of a lifetime.*

Why I received this gift I'll never know, as it isn't any of us who are running the show. All I will know is the pain of letting go, as this life is a temporary state and there is no time to waste in letting you know that I appreciate you both more than you'll ever know. You both gave me life which does have its strife, but taking the time to thank you is divine, and I thought you would like to know that I love you both so.

*Your child for infinity and with eternal love. I'm thankful to you both and to God from above. After all is said and done, it's all about **LOVE**.*

THE SYSTEMIC CONSTELLATION PROCESS

*T*his work can be approached in any number of ways. Some facilitate it based strictly on Bert Hellinger's original model. Others draw more on personal experience, letting intuition lead to adaptation. The "field" is wide open, if you will, and there are as many angles of approach as there are practitioners of this amazing modality. It goes by many names -- Family Constellation Work, Systemic Constellation Work, Trans-Generational Work -- yet, the premise is one and the same. Basically, the process helps us break certain family patterns that do not serve us. During the implementation of this work, a virtual lineage of background information is revealed, and the facilitator must be able to trust his or her own sensibilities with regard to interpreting this information as well as its sources. Therefore, although I highly recommend that everyone experience this work, attempting to facilitate it without proper training or certification is hereby implicitly discouraged. It's more, really, than just a matter of "Don't try this at home." This work presents a sacred opportunity -- one that shouldn't be taken lightly. It allows us the chance to permanently resolve any plaguing problem or issue by finding how its origin is hidden within the family system. In my opinion, it is a sacred process.

Constellations come in all shapes and sizes. In the night sky, some have a great many stars while others have relatively few. It is their configuration to each other, however, that gives the constellation its form. The same is true for familial constellations. It is our relationship to the other members of the system that creates the "big picture." In Trans-Generational work, a constellation process traditionally begins with the facilitator speaking with a client about the issue or problem that he or she would like to address. Even from this initial exchange, the aforementioned "field" of the client begins to reveal some of the hidden dynamics within their system. Although this modality takes place in a group setting, there is a wealth of information to be gathered during this personal process, and those experienced with energy work can pick up on such dynamics quite readily. While there are exceptions, the client is usually asked to choose someone to represent him or herself for the purpose of their constellation. If the chosen participant agrees to be a representative, the client then lightly touches him or her on the back and guides them into the circle, placing them wherever the client feels they belong. There is a "sacred contract" of sorts established when a client touches his or her representative's body. That human being who agrees to be of service to another holds tremendous value for the client, as well as the group as a whole. This process is repeated, as necessary, with the client choosing another representative for each person or element believed pertinent to the issue being addressed. That done, the client is able to sit back and observe how those representatives, including the one representing him or herself, interact with the other elements in the constellation. Sometimes it only takes a nanosecond for information to begin revealing itself. Other times, it may take a minute or two, depending on the sensibilities of the representatives and the willingness of the familial field. A word may suddenly come to mind. Perhaps there will be a subtle (or not-so-subtle) physical sensation. Even a lack of certainty can reveal information. Sometimes one person or element will feel uncomfortable near another. Sometimes a representative will suddenly feel tired, suddenly feel angry, or will find himself unexpectedly attracted to someone or some thing. Being able to read and utilize this information is the key to finding a simple, clear, concise resolution. The goal is not to intellectualize this process but, rather, to witness the energetic painting, if you will, that manifests before us. At times, this can include some pretty befuddling, archetypal energy. Yet, even if we do not cogently understand the significance of these revelations, the healing work is occurring nonetheless. It is an ever-changing, ever-morphing pictograph revealing the subtle truths and powerful emotions connected with the client's personal history and own inner process. Even without discussing these specifics with the facilitator, the energetic truth of the story behind the story is now revealed within the group setting. The new light shed by this information is always welcomed without any judgment whatsoever. It may involve rape. It may involve murder. It's still sacred information, and we approach it with dignity, respect and, yes, love. The client may be suffering because he or she is carrying something that isn't theirs to carry. Certainly, the pain needn't be theirs to carry. In such an instance, the goal might be to release the client from the repercussions wrought by those perceived "sins of the father," including feelings of guilt. This is accomplished by honoring and showing the ancestor respect, regardless of his or her deeds being good or bad. Again, it is not our place to judge. When we do, we attempt to make ourselves bigger than our ancestors, which dishonors the proper "order of love." They were part of the system before we were, perhaps having even passed on before we were born, yet their existence still has an energetic impact on us. By allowing ourselves to feel small and humble, we enable ourselves to ask for their help and, in turn, enable ourselves to receive it. Their unique energies impart valuable information that can benefit not only their relative, but the entire group, as well. So many levels of non-local realities manifest during this process that one can't help but look in awe at the power of the love that appears in the room, flowing from past generations to the present. As to the people picked at random to be representatives, there is often an issue within their own family system which they have in common with the client, despite its never having been discussed with the group. It is not unusual for someone who serves as a representative to find a healing within him or herself after participating in another's process. I consider this work, therefore, to be "holographic," reverberating at many levels within the group attending, both individually and collectively. In addition, this new flow of energy is not limited by walls or borders. If a living brother or uncle, for example, is represented in the process, any change that occurs on his behalf within the confines of the group will also begin to occur in the relative himself -- the real owner of the experience -- no matter where he may be. In other words, the healing effects are not confined to only that member of the system who is seeking help (meaning, the client), but are also felt throughout the system as a whole. Helping one piece of a puzzle find its place helps the entire puzzle to take shape. The same negative energies from which the client is released also loosen their grip on the entire system. It is an energetic "win-win" for all concerned. I liken it to tossing a pebble into a pond. The ripples reverberate out to every part of family system -- and beyond, depending on the issue on which the client is working. Again, ripples of energy know no boundaries of space or time, hence my "quantum physics" analogy. Of course, maybe this quantum link between all living things is precisely what makes this work possible. How else could the very essence of a deceased family member show up in the body of a total stranger who doesn't even know the client's last name? Why does a representative exude the identical symptoms of a physical ache that the person being represented had during his or her life? How can the very expression that an ancestor used enter a representative's vocabulary with no forehand knowledge? Perhaps our souls are more interconnected than we had ever imagined. What's more, this modality couldn't have come along at a better time. Helping us to see life's "bigger picture," it reminds us that our consciousness inhabits more than just a physical realm. As incredible as this work may sound, the information manifested is very real, utterly honest and quite profound. Furthermore, any type of issue can be addressed, not exclusively that which deals with familial concerns. Career choices, addictive behaviors, health problems, relationship issues, conflicts with business associates, even patterns of self-sabotage -- all topics are appropriate for this process, and vice versa. If a woman, for instance, has a question concerning a job opportunity, she might pick someone to represent herself, someone to represent her current job, and someone to represent the new job. Then she would be able to sit back and observe the interaction between these three elements. Perhaps the person representing her will begin to feel insecure and cling to the person representing the current job, or perhaps she will feel stronger the closer she stands to the representative of the new job. Regardless of the subject, the core dynamics always take us to the true heart of the issue, much like a spiral unraveling to reveal its center. As a result, even in instances where the client doesn't mention his or her family, their significance may still become evident. The "knowing field," as Hellinger calls it, will sometimes create a "role shift," where the representatives brought in as elements will suddenly start exhibiting familial traits. On the outset, a drama from days gone by may not seem to have much to do with the issue being addressed, but remember, this process takes us on a journey to the core of the conflict or question. In our job opportunity example, the person representing the woman's current job could have role shifted into representing her mother, revealing a parallel between career and familial dynamics. Perhaps the Mother/Current Job needs to say, "Go. Stand on your own two feet. You can feel secure without clinging to me." Of course, a facilitator well-trained in this work knows how to let the energy lead the way, trusting the field of awareness to unveil the true picture and not create a pre-conceived one. To coin a phrase, this process could be considered "archeology of the soul," helping us uncover those seed elements within the client's psyche that reveal what came before. Like the pieces of an energetic puzzle, they contain certain patterns that allow us to unify these fragments back into their intended state of wholeness. The tableaus created and movements made by the representatives help to illustrate where things first began to go astray within the system. By rearranging the puzzle pieces, if you will, the family members can be coaxed back into their proper, healthier "order of love." As a result, eons of negative charges built up around the issue's incompletion are released, which, in turn, frees the client to have a different association with that issue. Sometimes the changes are gradual; sometimes they are immediate. It all depends on the willingness of the field to show itself and, once the information is revealed, the willingness of the client to break the pattern and make a change. Most likely, the system has had years to become thus embroiled and may not be rushed to resolution, nor will the field be confined by the ego's determination of the issue. We are working with grand forces here, and they decide their own fates and destinies. As practitioners of this work, we are but their humble servants, discreetly encouraging a return of harmony and order where, for a while, there had been chaos and disassociation. Eliciting or accepting greater credit would simply be flirting with arrogance.

There are various ways of accessing and utilizing the field. Most facilitators practice this work in a traditional group setting, while others go "one on one" with the client. Some try to represent all the aspects themselves, while others draw the parts out on paper. Still others will use stick figures to represent the family members or elements being discussed. Regardless of the technique, the energies still come through. From speaking privately with the client, I am able to get a feel for what the core aspects are and make adjustments accordingly after the process has begun. I like to start simple, perhaps with just one person or element being represented, and then add on as the constellation dictates. Also, while I have lead many processes using the original Hellinger approach, I prefer to follow his later model for "blind" or concealed constellations -- that is, I prefer not to tell the various representatives who or what they are representing. By doing the work in this manner, no one is tempted to make up their own ego-fueled story about the subject or role they represent or filter the sensations or impulses based on what they think should be transpiring. In other words, if someone knows he is representing a father, for example, he may unknowingly begin to project his own father issues onto the role, thinking "a father would act this way" or "I bet his father acted that way." When only the client and the facilitator know who or what is being represented and by whom, it is easier to trust that what comes across is the true, unadulterated picture. This is especially important should the field start to transform it into a more detailed or entirely different portrait. As stated earlier, this energetic field is one of intelligence and clarity, and when we are open to its presence, it can depict a living landscape of the whole human family, not just the client's. In this state of awareness, the uttering of a simple phrase or the making of the slightest movement will create an energetic chain reaction traveling throughout and felt by every person within the room. When the truth is discerned, the energy generated is almost perceptible to the touch. This new level of consciousness allows us access to the true dynamics that are often hidden behind some neat and tidy story. Let's not forget, however, that such a story might have served a necessary purpose in the protection, insulation and ultimate survival of the family system. In a sense, it is the very essence of this work to love what may not have been loved and to INCLUDE what may have always been excluded. Again, this is a "no judgment" zone. A grandchild may not be versed in his or her familial history, and may not be aware of a lost child, a missing uncle, an insane aunt, an abortion, an accident or a murder -- yet those energies still live within that ever-knowing, ever-present field of consciousness. By allowing the field to guide us, rather than vice versa, we allow it room to transform itself, which, in turn, allows us to see something positive where before we perceived only negative.

Call it what you like -- sense memory, soul, spirit, psyche, collective unconscious, inner awareness or just a gut feeling. It is all as valid as the diverse descriptions we give it. It also has to be respected for its duality. Remember, the same force that created the light also created the dark. Everything is unified and balanced through perpetual change and forward motion. Teachings such as the Kabbalah address this notion, as well. This is also the context in which Bert Hellinger approaches his work. Transformation and change don't occur unless opposing forces act upon or as a result of one another. Death nourishes life as life nourishes death. We do not need to judge one as better or worse than the other. Humans are also all equal in this regard. We all live and we all die. It doesn't get any more simple than that.

In the Trans-Generational process, we are accessing the family system's consciously unconscious life force. By bringing to light what was hidden, we can profoundly reshape our perceptions of our so-called issues. When I lead various workshops in America, I call the lecture portion "Shift Happens," for that seems to summarize the results of this work most concisely and colloquially. Not only is there a shift in the energy flow within the family system, there is an important and significant shift in perception, as well. This allows the changes begun in the workshop setting to continue long after the process has ended. Furthermore, even those family members not present and who have no knowledge of this work will, nonetheless, find themselves affected by it, as they are part of the same system. I cannot tell you the number of times a client has reported a sibling or other relative suddenly phoning the day after a constellation in which an energetic shift was experienced on their behalf. Even without doing this work directly, all members of the system become transformed in one way or another. In addition, many representatives have noticed their own issues resolving just by being present in someone else's process. Needless to say, something big is going on here. The cathartic release of energy we may not have even known we were carrying is quite profound to say the least. The family story may have been one of pain, sadness, anger, mistrust, shame, insecurity, lust, guilt, or any other emotion or combinations thereof. With this work, we are genuinely opening Pandora's Box; but, unlike the old tale, the negatives we release here actually dissipate or transform into something positive. Basically, there is simply more to any story than we realize. Fortunately, the field seems to know just how much truth we can take at any given time, and it administers the proper dosage accordingly. Since this process functions at an energetic level, it is best to let the shifts take root after the constellation and not force any potential change back into the cerebral, ego realm by overanalyzing what has just transpired. In other words, let it be. We are changed from the inside out rather than outside in. Remember, we don't have to carry what isn't ours to bear. To ensure that we do not, we must believe that our forefathers and mothers did the best job they possibly could given their circumstances, which were probably a lot more challenging than ours. Everyone's life has its joys, its sorrows and its pains. We are all thrown various curve balls at one time or another. Although it is incredibly easy and convenient to do so, it is also extremely arrogant of us to sit in judgment of our elders. This one simple act of disrespect is what skews the essential "order of love" and sets off a domino effect of dysfunction throughout the entire family system. Again, Hellinger has observed the importance of being "little" compared to those who came before us. By letting them remain "larger than life," we allow ourselves to be vulnerable and, therefore, open to receive. Of course, it is very easy to get "out of order," if you will, when we identify more with a grandparent, let's say, than with our own father or mother. During puberty, for example, it is not at all uncommon to develop certain feelings of resentment toward our own parents, allowing other loyalties within the family system to become established. While they may serve as an important catalyst in our maturity, these feelings of superiority will harden and create a systemic blockage, so to speak, if carried into adulthood. Trans-generationally, it behooves us to recognize that we will always be our parents' children, even after becoming parents ourselves. This is why it is so vital that we keep that "order of love" flowing properly.

With each new generation, our familial roles are expanded. Children become parents. Parents become grandparents. The smallest member has a great impact on the "bigger" ones, creating a huge event in the family system's history simply by being born and, simultaneously, helping them to feel small in comparison to those bigger forces perpetuating the whole system. In other words, never underestimate the power of a baby. Even an abortion or miscarriage alters the family system forever. Having a clear understanding of our own place in the systemic order, therefore, enables us to better cope when certain events, both expected and otherwise, create change in our lives. This clarity should exist with regard to the birth order of siblings, as well. Someone may have always been led to believe, for example, that he is the eldest child in the family. If his mother, however, miscarried a child before he was born, he would actually have been the second child in that womb and, energetically, the second child in his family system. Systemically, this is important information. By denying that first child his or her place in the family, the parents may be passing the energetic buck, so to speak, to the first "born." Subconsciously, he may begin to demonstrate an affinity for the macabre or even develop serious health problems as a way of showing a loyalty of sorts to his older, forgotten sibling. If my experiences with trans-generational processes are any indication, this precise scenario is actually far more common than one might imagine. Bottom line: your place in your family system's "order of love" is yours and yours alone. No one else can fill it, and it is yours for all eternity. Even when the "baby" of the family eventually becomes a great grandmother, she will still be the "baby" of her original family's system. It really isn't as tangled a web as it may seem. No matter how jumbled or convoluted the system may have become, order can be restored with just a little effort and trust. Sometimes asking for help can be remarkably empowering.

I often see clients who are more than just a little willing to describe their families as "dysfunctional." While, to an extent, this assessment may be accurate, it is also not an altogether helpful perception to embrace. I prefer to think of such a family system as having actually been rather successful. After all, it succeeded in getting the client to this point, here, in the present, where he or she is asking for some help. No matter what drawbacks there may have been, the system achieved its goal of getting the next generation into adulthood. The rest is really window dressing. We may never fully understand how some decisions were made with regard to our upbringing, but, then again, perhaps they were never ours to understand. We need to remain "small" regarding our childhood, and let the adult decisions remain with those who were adults. This is part of what makes the Hellinger process so amazing. It provides us access to the inner workings of the system at large while still allowing us to retain our "smallness." Accepting things as they were -- good, bad or indifferent -- is all that we can do. As powerless as we may be to change the facts, we certainly needn't be victimized by our perceptions of them. Truth be told, this is perhaps the hardest and yet most important "pattern" to break. Hellinger observes, as you'll recall, that, on some deep level, we have agreed to pay a price to be part of the system into which we were born. Once we recognize this covert aspect of human nature, we can release ourselves from the ego's belief that things could-a, would-a, should-a been different. They weren't. We often try, however, to relive or recreate the past by seeking what is familiar -- including misery. Even as children, we unconsciously agree to help carry the load or burden for our family out of great love. There was a time, though, when I resisted this idea. "How could I," I thought, "a severely abused child, have agreed to that?" I was, after all, a victim. I kept referring to myself, thinking of myself, defining myself as a victim. In fact, I wore my "victimhood" as if it were a red badge of courage. Then a shift happened. I had heard of this new modality called Trans-Generational Constellation Work, and I decided to give it a try. During my constellation process, I found myself becoming stronger and stronger. It was a strange sensation, yet there was something familiar as well, something that filled my eyes with unexpected tears. There I was, in the NOW, and my perception had completely changed. I saw that, as a child, my love had actually been so strong for my parents -- these people I was sure I hated -- that I was determined to prove to them that I could take whatever abuse they could give, just as they had "taken it" when they had been children. Out of an unconscious loyalty to their own parents, they were, of course, repeating a familial pattern. Cruel as it may have seemed, this is how they shared an experience from their own childhoods with me, and I felt it my duty to accept, out of love, what I perceived as an unavoidable challenge. As I stood there in my first constellation process, how proud I was that it had ended there, that I had not become a perpetrator myself, and that the pattern of abuse had been broken -- or so I thought. Then, another shift happened. I began to see that, unknowingly, I actually had kept the pattern going deep within myself. For decades after my father had died, I still felt as if I were being victimized. Then it dawned on me: I do still feel like a victim, only now **I have become my perpetrator.** I believe I literally fell to my knees. I was stunned. If I didn't have to be a victim anymore, who was I? At first, I couldn't process the possibilities. All I could do was bask in the moment, letting this new-found, positive energy fill me to the brim. Years later, as a facilitator of this incredible work, I realize just how much we deny ourselves, all the while thinking that someone else is doing it to us. I had always believed I hated my parents, that I felt no loyalty to them whatsoever. Now I see that I had actually been going to great lengths to maintain my victim status, and that I subconsciously believed their treatment of me had been correct and somehow deserved. Again, Hellinger has found that the Gift of Life we receive from our parents is so great that we may feel we need to pay some price in exchange. In reality, though, all we need to do is simply see them for who they were and honor them, thereby seeing and honoring that part of ourselves. In the big scheme of things, that's the greatest "thank you" we can give.

We live at a most fortunate time in human history. We are afforded comforts and conveniences that our ancestors never were able to enjoy. Mere survival was a predominate concern during the Great Depression. The servicemen and women of both World War I and World War II were similarly focused on daily "life-or-death" situations. Perhaps our forebears had to flee their native countries in search of safety and sustenance. Such trauma and turmoil left those generations little time for speculation about systemic patterns or familial order. Their devotion and sacrifice, however, is what has enabled us to pursue the lifestyles we enjoy today, including the opportunity to explore these inner workings of the human psyche. It occurred to me recently that had those Nazi soldiers not "given" their lives to my father in the second World War, I may never have been born. As a member of the "baby boomer" generation, I would have never existed had he been killed instead. As part of nature's divine balancing act, this great loss of life was followed by a great resurgence. Looking at the bigger picture, perhaps I also owe my existence to those millions of Jews who perished in the great genocide wrought by that most infamous of perpetrators himself, Adolph Hitler. Perhaps the tremendous death toll in Europe and the murderous energy needed to survive in such wartime gave my father the impetus to see that life would continue -- a desire from which I have unquestionably benefited. In hindsight, how dare I judge him? This is how thinking we are "bigger" than our parents can get us into karmic trouble. At this late stage of my life, I have finally learned how to honor him and his suffering, so I needn't continue to carry it as his son. Again, when you allow yourself to be little and humble, you are able to feel as vulnerable as that child you might never have gotten to finish being. In other words, this process allows you to energetically "grow up" into a much wiser and more compassionate son or daughter. Hellinger observes that in addition to being able to say, "You were the best parents for me," we need to be able to feel it, as well. The past can't be undone. It doesn't have to be. What this work does provide, however, is the opportunity to get back to that place inside ourselves that is still priceless and new, to let ourselves fully receive this great gift we've been given, and to finally see how we continue to hurt ourselves far more than any parent could ever have. A "mindset of victimization" gets passed down the generational line as easily as brown eyes or red hair. Unconsciously, we agree to carry this negativity for those who lived before us, yet wallowing in the residue of a time that no longer exists is one of the biggest disservices we can do ourselves. Of course, perpetrator and victim are two opposite edges of the same behavioral sword. This is what makes this particular family pattern so very hard to break. Feeling victimized as children teaches us to become perpetrators as adults, even if our victim isn't always someone else. And yet, we do have a choice. We can admit that it's time to grow up, take charge, and be adults by putting a stop to our own suffering. Otherwise, we can become sixty-year-old brats, whining about what victims we are -- in essence, fighting to remain immature. I realize that taking a stand for my own life and accepting that my past "is what it is" was actually one of the most empowering things I could have ever done. It brought me "up to date," so to speak, and into the all-important NOW. The past may be a nice place to visit but, as the saying goes, "you wouldn't want to live there." At least, we really shouldn't. Still, it is not our place to judge those who may continue to hold the "victim" banner high, for they truly believe it is their duty to serve the family system in that way. Perhaps, instead, we should stop and thank that family member for carrying the familial burden on his or her shoulders so that we can have what they feel they cannot. What if we thanked him for his self-sacrifice or tried congratulating her for being in service to her other siblings? By altering our perception of their behaviors, we cause an alteration in the energetic flow within the system, creating that "ripple" effect felt throughout the entire family. As a result of such positive recognition, they may no longer feel the need to carry the weight in order to feel that they are included, thus enabling them to surrender their "martyr" status. In other words, a little honor and respect can do wonders for the living as well as the deceased.

Although others within the family system derive residual benefits from the energetic shifts that occur, this work best serves those who take a proactive approach to feeling better about themselves or improving their situations. Again, we do not have to sacrifice our own lives for the unfinished business of our ancestors. What we can do, however, is work to resolve our own issues, which are likely rooted in theirs. By altering our part of the historical pattern, we inherently alter theirs as well, thereby allowing new possibilities to emerge from the ashes of the old. One of the qualities that intrigued me most about this work was the notion that our deceased loved ones can actually offer us help from the "other side." Most of us, I believe, understand that feeling when someone we were close to in life continues to "inspire" us, if you will, despite their having passed on. Hellinger has observed that, when invited to do so, such energies are quite willing to take an active role within the context of the constellation process. The idea that specific, valuable information can be supplied by an unseen, familial essence is rather mind-boggling to say the least. Yet, this work is to and from the heart, not the mind. In case after case, I have seen and heard the personality and speech patterns of a specific family member resonate from the total stranger who is representing him or her. Sometimes, as I've mentioned before, a "role shift" may even occur, morphing the perceived issue into the one that actually needs to be addressed in order for change to take place. It is as if our loved ones come to help free us from the unnecessary ties that bind us to the past -- their past -- or to the issue that we think embodies our ancestral history. By doing so, we are able to fully live in the present, unconstrained by their fate or the confines of their experience.

FULL CIRCLE

We all get our chance to shine in the sun
before our time ends and our destiny's done,
as we meet those who came before in the bigger field of death
to be rejoined with them in spirit once again.
The cycle completes itself yet again -- nothing lost,
everything gained as life experiences life yet again.
Life goes on unto its death. The wind of the living
fills our breath
until it stops, then we encounter death as we meet
with the others
who gave us the breath as we follow them back
into their death
where we are all united as one under the eternal sun
with the mysteries of life understood and learned
from the invisible forces that feed all existence.
To understand life is to come "**Full Circle.**"

It is through the awe-inspiring sacredness of this work that this is able to happen. It is as if the large "knowing field" is able to select -- from all the information contained within the universe -- that which is needed to resolve the issue being addressed. This energy is so facile in its "knowledge," if you will, that facts previously unknown to the client are often revealed.

I have experienced this many times both as a representative and as a facilitator. When that family member inevitably researches the newly-discovered information, ("Did I have an uncle who drowned?" or "Mom, did you have two miscarriages before I was born?") the revelations are proven to be uncannily accurate. It seems as if our familial field has a will of its own -- a desire, so to speak, to complete something unfinished so that its great granddaughter or grandson, for example, can live a full and unencumbered life. As such, many secrets come out in the process. Again, it is important to welcome all information without judgment or censure. Someone working on a career issue, for instance, may find himself uncovering evidence of multi-generational sexual abuse. Someone working on an addiction issue may discover an "illegitimate" pregnancy in the family line. In more instances than you might imagine, matters of paternity involving other members of the family, including Grandpa, are often revealed. For some reason, much of this energy seems to emanate from the late nineteenth or early twentieth century. One can speculate about the degree of repression during this point in human history, but it matters not so long as the current family members are released from the entanglements of those past events. Never forget, however, that had those events not transpired, that grandchild might not be here today. Such speculation can be applied to each and every family, including our own. This is why life seems to me to be an undulating, amoebic-like entity that seeks out ways to recreate itself as it passes through time, hormonally fueled by love and/or lust. The fact that such procreative forces ultimately yield positive results, however, does not preclude the existence of certain common traits that bind us negatively to our ancestors. Archetypal energies that defy explanation often manifest during the process. Again, such occurrences need not satisfy our "rational" minds. We need only hold that some divine drama is finally playing itself out, allowing room for a new scenario written by the client him or herself. When the sacred moment occurs -- when the aspect that had created tension within the representatives' bodies has been released or transformed -- an inner feeling of peace and calmness is inexplicably yet undeniably experienced by everyone in attendance. While, in some ways, we are in control, it is also more than a little humbling to witness just how we are not. It is in the acceptance of this precise paradox that the resolution is revealed to us. In a sense, the "knowing field" is analogous to an atom seeking to transfer a negative electron to another atom, thereby creating a combination never before known. The energetic field of those who came before us contains a… well, a "holy" quality, if you will, transcending any one religion. There is, I believe, a bigger intelligence at work, not only within each family system, but within the entire familial system of humanity, as well. When what has been unseen or unspoken is finally acknowledged and included as part of our existence, our negative perceptions are allowed to dissipate or transform into positive ones. In other words, they can no longer subconsciously control us when we are consciously in control of them. Once that correct and proper "order of love" has been re-established, we can be free to live our own lives and have our own experiences -- instead of recreating someone else's.

BASIC DEFINITIONS AND USAGE
OF TRANS-GENERATIONAL TERMS

Father: A man starts the Family System when he marries or fathers a child.

Mother: She bears the children and continues the birth line of both families.

Children: They establish the continuation of each family system and shift the roles of everyone who came before (from child to parent to grandparent to great grandparent, etc.) Each child born establishes the birth order (oldest to youngest) of all the siblings to follow. As a rule, children take and parents give until the children become parents of their own.

Bonding: A connection is formed when a couple has a child (if not before). They bond first then the children bond with the family group, who bond with other members within the family system until they begin another generation. In most cases, the bond between mother and child is the strongest. There are also strong nationalistic bonds or those with one's country of origin that remain unbroken by emigration or relocation. Americans often unite as one -- a concept on which this nation was founded. (E Pluribus Unum)

Reaching Out: This movement of a child to its parents denotes a desire to be loved and hugged. If this movement is interrupted, the child may spend a lifetime wondering why: What did I do wrong? Why aren't I loved? Every bond thereafter may be questioned or seem incomplete. (Adoption issues)

Hierarchy: This refers to the birth order among siblings and the generational order of parent, grandparent, great grandparent and needs to be respected and honored. This order remains consistent, yet expands to include its newest member.

Family System: Our family of origin and the family we create are all part of an extended system spanning many generations.

Constellation: A grouping of seemingly separate elements which, given their relationship to one another, form a "bigger" picture.

Conscience: Each system has its own beliefs and its own "conscience," and it strives to be maintained, especially when systems merge through marriage. A wife's family's belief system may be very different from her husband's and the clash of those systems may impact their union. (Remember Romeo & Juliet?) Sometimes a wife, for example, remains loyal to her family system, thereby excluding her husband's (or vice versa). Ultimately, the pair needs to start a new system with its own conscience and beliefs.

Loyalty: This is part of the bonding process within the system. Sometimes this can refer to a child being loyal to its mother over the father or vice versa. Sometimes a loyalty may lie between systems, meaning the person isn't fully emotionally available to either, much like when a body is present but the heart and mind are elsewhere.

Feelings: The full array of all human emotions. The primal or core feelings lie deeper and can be masked by our reactions.

Anger, for instance, can cover up deep sadness over rejection, as sadness can cover deep anger.

Taking our Place: We all belong to the family, even those who may not have been treated as such. We all have a place, and restoring it restores our relationships, as well. (Divorces, deaths, remarriages, etc.)

Exclusion: This is one of the most damaging yet most common retaliations that can happen within a family system. This refers to any situation where someone is left out, forgotten, ignored, or forbidden to be part of the group for any reason. (Divorce, economic status, sexual orientation, suspicion or commitment of a crime, jealously, death)

Entanglement: This occurs when anyone within the family system becomes identified with someone else, within or outside of the system. This identification is usually negative in nature because it is out of the true family order. For instance, a granddaughter may be linked negatively to her grandmother if she exhibits contempt for her own mother, treating her like a child when she (the daughter) is really the child. This creates a disturbance in the hierarchy and in the "order of love." Such entanglements could also be passed down from the "great greats" in their example of how mothers and daughters bond or do not bond, as the case may be. Entanglements may also be connected to some disease that pervades the family system, labeled as "genetic" when, in fact, it may bespeak an emotional incompletion of some other trauma never resolved within the system. Depression, cancer, sexually transmitted diseases, heart disease, even violent acts committed to or by a member of the system can entangle the victim or perpetrator into the other family system, as well. There are also generational entanglements where a child identifies with an unfinished drama or represents someone excluded in an attempt to include them or to remind the system of that missing one.

Primal: Raw and fundamental, as in the base emotion found at the core of an issue. Feelings of such a primitive nature are often repressed. Constellation work provides a safe outlet for their expression and release.

Tension: This refers to the unacknowledged energy or the unspoken words or feelings that need completion in order for inner peace to be attained. If an issue is not resolved, this quality takes the place of such peace. Unfinished business creates an energetic tension in the family field. Such negative energy can become disease when the patterns or issues get passed down to the future generation to resolve. A good marker for knowing when the work is complete is when the tension dissipates and a feeling of relaxation ensues.

Paradox: A situation or statement that seems inconsistent but is not, such as, "We are all unique, yet we are all the same." In this work, such polarity of perspective is appreciated as part of the great mystery of life.

Constellation Process: A way to access the hidden dynamics through group or individual work with a client who wants some help with an area of his or her life. Such access can be attained in any number of ways.

Knowing Field: An energetic field of knowledge representing all or part of the client's family system. It manifests so that harmony and order may replace chaos and incompletion. Defying space and time, it could be thought of as "quantum" or consciousness in its rawest form. Its intelligence and energetic qualities are actually palpable. Transcending life and death, it is essentially healing in nature and very sacred and needs to be honored and respected, for the information revealed benefits all concerned.

The Great Mystery: As humans, we try to attach positive or negative values to things we do not comprehend. In this work, we stay neutral and do not judge the bigger forces that created death and turmoil, hate and war. They simply are, and we deal with the effects in line with the individual and collective fates of those involved. We should remember that the "divine drama" is trying to teach us something. We are just observers watching its effects and attempting to restore harmony or resolve something incomplete.

God: All definitions are valid. All are equal. None is better than the others.

Acceptance: This means seeing whatever truth is shown or just accepting the fate or destiny of the group or individual without regret. By letting go of past events that can never be changed, we can change the future.

Humility: This is how we allow ourselves to be "little," not knowing what we thought we did. This helps us "give in" to and, ultimately, be at one with the unknown forces that rule our destiny.

Love: This word can paint very broad strokes across the family system. Its palate can include issues of sexuality, pain, remorse, joy, sadness, longing, violence, hope, ill health, self-hatred, loyalties, and disloyalties. Love is what makes us want to try to get better, and to share that health with others.

Honoring: By no longer resisting the familial "order of love" and thanking those who came before us, we are better able to participate in life and disengage from unhealthy patterns established within the system. Honoring our parents and our fate is a good place to start. Allowing ourselves to see, hear and feel the "good' rather than judging the "bad" (which weakens us) gives us the strength to create our own destinies. It is also a sign of respect for and acceptance of things that cannot be changed.

Embracing: To embrace or accept what we dislike in others (especially our parents) allows order to be restored and releases us from the patterns set within the system. This pertains to that which we dislike about ourselves, as well. What we hate seems to grow. What we embrace is free to go.

Forgiveness: Unlike most spiritual practices of present day, this work does NOT encourage us to forgive others as this act of "bigness" forces us to carry weight that is not ours, further perpetuating disorder. Our parents are adults who have the strength to carry the responsibility of their own actions. We do not have to take on what is not ours to carry. We are adults letting them be adults in return, having them carry their own weight and be responsible for their own fate. This way, we are not victims either.

Victim/Perpetrator: It is so very important to discover just who the real victim was, as well as the possible *hidden perpetrator*. Things are not always what they seem, and the official story may cover up the "energetic" reality of the situation, especially with regard to cases of exclusion. There are also instances of violence where the roles shift as instantaneously as the shot of a gun, making the victim the real perpetrator and the blamed perpetrator the victim. Again, they are the two edges of the same systemic sword. Beware and be sensitive.

Rejection: The right to belong is sometimes impinged by the group. Nevertheless, it is a birthright that cannot be undone, no matter how smug or "successful" the family may think it has been. Gay, lesbian and trans-gendered family members are often prime targets for exclusion. We each have our place in the family system, however, and no one else can fill it.

Movement of the Soul: There is information contained within the physical movements of the representatives during a constellation process. Remember, the undulating field of consciousness wants to move toward fulfillment and find completion. A child or parent may energetically reach out to bond. The dead may bestow the needed encouragement to move on with life or to go on living. Regardless of the words spoken, physical movement can provide a deeper picture and hold the key to understanding the hidden truth within any situation.

Grief: This is one of the most discombobulating feelings humans carry in response to misfortune, particularly with regard to the death of a loved one. If such feelings are not dealt with and released in the proper generation, they can be passed down to the next or recreated by the next in order to find resolution. The shock of the sudden loss of a child, for example, can cripple the heart of a mother. Instead of allowing herself to fully feel the pain of the situation, she may turn her grief to anger or blame herself or the father. The familial message "Do not trust men" may get passed down the ancestral line, when the real issue was "I lost my baby."

TRANS-GENERATIONAL QUESTIONS TO THINK ABOUT

The following questions are intended to jog your memory of important events that may have shaped and affected your family system in some way. Character and personality traits or personal interests are not the focus of this work, but the events that shaped those concerned may be.

FAMILY of ORIGIN: These questions relate to your siblings, your parents and their siblings (all uncles & aunts), the grandparents and, in cases where they might have had a dramatic or tragic event in their lives, (such as a death at childbirth) the great grandparents, as well as any premarital partners of your parents and grandparents.

PRESENT FAMILY: These questions also relate to any former partners and any children from a former marriage or relationship.

Is there anything that happened in your present family or your family of origin that was tragic or unusual?

Did anyone in your family:
* die at a young age?

(Did a partner or a child of yours die? Did your father, mother or sibling die when you were young? Did a parent or sibling of your parents die when your parents were still young?)

* **die during childbirth?**
* suffer from an illness or disability from having given birth to a child? (Your mother, grandmother, great grandmother or a former partner of your father or grandfather)
* Did your mother or grandmother find her life in danger during childbirth?
* **commit suicide?**
* die in action as a soldier or kill others as a result of a war?

Did you or anyone in your family ever:
* have a stillborn child?
* have an abortion or miscarriage? (Both of these types of events can affect a couple's relationship but may not have as great an impact on the children. Children should not inquire about an abortion or miscarriage, but should honor it as part of their parents' private relationship. A stillborn child IS considered a sibling and the other children would do well to know about it.)
* have a so-called "illegitimate" child?
* have a child that was abandoned or given up for adoption?
* **have a former spouse, fiancé, partner or lover of either gender?**
  (Parents or grandparents) Children should inquire about former partners only if they were a spouse or fiancé. Other kinds of relationships are part of the parent's privacy. However, children should know about other children from ANY former relationship.
* have a serious illness?
* have a long-lasting illness?

* have a physical or mental disability?
* attempt suicide?
* commit a crime(s)?
* commit a war crime? (Children should not inquire about this.)
* survive (or not survive) the Holocaust?
* become a missing person?
* join the clergy or enter a monastery?
* encounter prejudice or slander or experience being treated with contempt or as an outcast: (gay or lesbian family members, disabled persons, alcoholics, criminals)?
* complain about being taken advantage of? (such as with regard to an inheritance)?
* find yourself or themselves ignored, not respected or not honored?
* emigrate to another country?
* lose your or their fortune?
* Not marry and so be belittled?
* live an unusual life?
* disappear for a while?
* feel like the "black sheep" of the family?
* experience being "disowned?"
* feel ostracized or excluded for any reason whatsoever?

Important events in the area of personal experience:
These include events such as a difficult or Cesarean birth, separation from the mother at a young age (such as for an extended hospital stay), traumatic experiences in childhood, life-threatening events or accidents at any age. A variety of symptoms may result, but they may not be considered systemic entanglements unless there is a history that is repeated across generations.

These topics for self-reflection are included so that, as you read the rest of this book, you may think in more "systemic terms" about your own family system and retain a deeper understanding of the historical events that have helped to shape your life.

ENTANGLEMENTS

A long with the natural and healthy bonding that occurs in any family system, there are also hidden links and alliances formed between the child and the inner issues of the parent, communicated nonverbally yet with unmistakable clarity. Perhaps it is the child's innocence that allows him or her to readily absorb every energetic aspect of its creators. Perhaps it is contingent on his sensitively to the unspoken, unseen issues that surround him within the energetic field of the larger family system. Sometimes the child may have an unconscious mission to represent a missing person or someone excluded by death or unexpressed grief. The child, therefore, may unknowingly emulate the excluded person's life in a karmic effort to bring the system back into balance. It is as if the unconditional love that a child has for the family will seek out various jobs to do, as if to say, "Thank you for giving me life." Unconsciously, he or she may be saying, "I'll hold your pain about the loss of your fiancé or the exclusion of your dead uncle." This can pertain to the issues of either parent, mother or father. Despite their innocence, children will intuitively take note of the "sore spots" within the family system and will latch onto them as a way of sharing the burden with the parents, not realizing the damage they are doing to themselves by taking on more life than they can effectively handle. Remember, a child's love for his or her creators is boundless and unconditional. In a case where a bitter divorce, for instance, has yielded a rejected grandparent, the child may take on the job of finding out who this missing loved one is, thereby bringing their memory back into the family field in an attempt to make it complete again. This process may even concern a deceased relative whom the child has never met. Most likely, there is a negative emotional charge regarding this missing ancestor fueled by unreleased grief or anger. The child may pick up on those elements and may repeat the same type of events that led to the exclusion, or even the death. Ultimately, the child seeks to include everyone to make it "one big, happy family." On some naïve yet profoundly acute level, the child knows that there really is enough for all. Of course, it is quite amazing that a child could try to fulfill the role of someone he or she has not met but who was (or is) a part of the bigger family system. Yet, that is precisely what happens. If the child is identified with, say, his maternal grandfather whom he may have never met, the child might act more like a father to his mother through the power of that entanglement with the previous generation. Unconsciously, her son's behavior will seem somehow familiar to her and will, most likely, push her familial "buttons," perhaps reminding her of some unresolved issues she has with her father, thereby causing her to react to her son as if she were once again a little girl. You can see how such a scenario, in and of itself, can create disharmony within the family, as the child isn't being a child but, rather, is acting "too big for his britches," feeling superior to his own parents because of this identification with a bigger, older, senior family force. Such a case denotes merely the start of a lifetime entanglement -- an ongoing dynamic that is neither healthy for the individual family members nor the system as a whole. Through the Primal Constellation process, we can identify and, subsequently, alter the energy trapped in such behavior by giving the disconnected relative his proper place, thereby restoring the "order of love" within the system by eliminating the negative identification. Such entanglements are often behind a child's precociousness... or downright obnoxiousness. It's so amazing how a "new being" can feel such a connection to family members he or she has never met, and yet the personality traits of these excluded people, the missing and the dead, will be emulated with shocking accuracy. Although the entanglement process does not seem to serve the developmental health of the child, perhaps learning about life through the family prism of collective experiences is what our "consciousness" is there to teach us. While it, in one sense, robs the child of his or her innocence, it also fulfills the child as being a member (and future adult) of the system that gave him or her life. Perhaps this is part of how we learn to give and take -- a good life lesson to employ in adulthood, as well. Sometimes we learn the most by what hurts us the most. Of course, one of the most debilitating aspects of entanglements is the distorted view of life they create. Such folks often feel distrustful of people and may have resentments about those in positions of authority. They may suddenly and inexplicably feel that they are in an "unsafe" situation and that they must avoid it if they are to survive. Again, such family members are not so much reacting to the NOW as they are reenacting the preprogrammed responses to situations that pertained to other generations. Needless to say, this is not the healthiest or the most objective lens through which to view the world. A child trying to function within the confines of his immediate family while simultaneously carrying a memory or feeling that is not his own may feel quite conflicted indeed. Remember, when the child acts "bigger" than the parents, those parents often revert back to being victimized children themselves, since the child, entangled with a grandparent, may remind them of their own unresolved childhood issues. Hence, the parents never grow up while the child becomes too grown up, which could also be a generational pattern passed down within the family system. The family order, therefore, remains askew, and every subsequent generation of children and parents are robbed of their corresponding childhoods and adulthoods. Welcome to the wonderful world of dysfunctional family dynamics with which we are all too familiar. Of course, I want to stress again that I am not judging any of this as "bad" or "wrong." It is simply, perhaps, not ideal. The optimum and correct order of love, however, can be restored to the family system. This is what the Trans-Generational process is all about. Regardless of anyone's belief concerning the immediate or previous generations in your family system, their success lies within you, as you are alive and here and in the NOW. As I've said before, the rest is just window-dressing. Our problems may seem like the end of the world, but they are not. Life goes on, and our family systems go on. This is why it is so important to release any personal traumas or frustrations, rather than allowing them to inhibit the future of the next generation. Still, it is out of love and duty to the larger system that parents continue to pass along, nonverbally, those life lessons they received from their parents who, of course, passed along the experiences transferred to them from their parents.

Life is never really lost, only lessons gained!

All things -- the good and the seemingly bad -- get passed down along with that gift of life from the ancestors. Now, thanks to the discoveries and observations of Bert Hellinger, we have an effective way to deal with our family's historical, yet unfinished, business. We now have a profound, energetic window, if you will, through which to peer into the "quantum" past, helping us to better understand those issues from another time and another place. We can witness, first hand, the original stimuli that created the responses that still exist within our family systems today. The Primal Constellation process allows us to "holographically" interact within the system's back-story that lives within the present moment, thereby allowing us to discover the real cause of those unconscious dynamics that may have been hidden by a family story that was... less than true, let us say. Again, those stories may serve a higher purpose, though, in protecting some members from the real horror of what may have actually happened so that the group could face another day of life together. Remember, "survival" is the key for all living things. Even if the systemic state of balance was imperfection, that was fine, as the mission was accomplished for the good of the whole. "One for all and all for one," as they say. Everything we humans do is ultimately for love. We will do anything for it, even harm ourselves if we think it will somehow benefit the system. We will unconsciously consent to be victimized for the very same reason. We will endure any type of suffering during our incarnation in order to experience "love." The irony, of course, is that we really don't have to suffer at all. Still, since many of us have, there is great relief in knowing that those perceived mistakes actually turned out alright after all. No matter what happened or what we believe happened in our family system's past, all was ultimately done for love, and we survived it. We can find great inner peace by dropping the pretense that things could have or should have happened another way. They didn't, and we can save ourselves a lifetime of aggravation and despair if we can accept it all as it was and not get stuck on how it "should have been."

Nevertheless, let me reiterate the importance of identifying and releasing ourselves from those negative entanglements we have with other members of our family system. By failing to do so, we are merely sweeping it under the generational rug, so to speak, and the next generation is sure to find it there. Again, a child who over-identifies with a grandparent may begin to show contempt for his or her own parents, a dynamic which could also be part of the generational pattern. Since these behaviors and attitudes follow us into the adult world, they create the potential for other dysfunctional relationships with employers, spouses, authority figures, and anyone else with whom we may deal on a daily basis. We internalize our childhood perceptions, and they have a seemingly unavoidable and lifelong effect. They are how we perpetuate the template of what we learned from our family system onto the world at large, thereby reinforcing our beliefs on how the world is supposed to work. As adults, we often attempt to recreate what is familiar to us, projecting our family dynamics on different situations or encounters throughout our lives. Let me use an example from my own life. My father developed a malignant cancer at a rather young age, his early forties, just as I was entering my teens. After his passing, I unconsciously tried to fill that familial void left by the missing parent, as I was the oldest sibling and the only boy, as well. In a way, I was trying to comfort my mother in her grief and, at the same time, be a role model for my younger sisters. Basically, I was trying to take over the role of the father. It is quite painful to observe, in hindsight, how I had to split myself in two to make up the difference for a lost father in a family of seven living just at the borderline of poverty. Painful, also, because I see that I was actually doing it out of love for a family system that I thought I hated. Again, the ultimate motivation was survival, even if it was at my own psychological expense. Fast-forward to my adult self many years later. Wherever I see a void, I try to fill it even if it is not my responsibility to do so, whether it be a work or social situation. I'll do double time to pick up the slack even if I'm not asked to do so. Frankly, I have become a "workaholic." What's more, I have discovered that I often resent having to do so much, and would unconsciously resent others for not working as hard. Of course, this behavior was rooted in the loss of my father. This teenage template was welded to my personality through grief and tragedy, setting up a pattern which I willingly internalized. Only now am I beginning to see how I would project this onto any situation whether it be in society, at work or at home. It scares me to see how I recreate and react to the same external stimuli that affected me so in those formative years which were beyond my control. I know now that I subconsciously did it for love and that I self-sacrificed out of what I perceived as a sense of duty to my family. I also know that I was not and am not the victim I once felt I was and would always be. I am now able to carry the responsibility for my own fate. Had I discovered Hellinger's Trans-Generational process years ago, I could have saved myself decades of confusion, resentment and self-doubt. My relationship with my father was strained at best, fraught with much fear and trepidation from being a battered child; I was greatly relieved at his passing knowing I would never again be beaten. Still, I did my very best to care for the family he had helped to create. This is but one example of how a child can become "bigger" than his parents. I was simply trying to fill a tragic void left by a sudden death at the head of the family. I had really not grasped what had actually transpired until I became aware of the hidden dynamics at work during one of my first constellation processes. I was stunned to discover how much I truly loved my father. For years, I had been telling myself a different story. Within the context of the "knowing field," however, a different set of energetic truths were revealed. Organically, this process creates its own expression of the family system's hidden energy in its entirety. Seeing and feeling this unfold in front of me allowed me to revert back to a time when I was truly little, before I began to play my adult/child role. For the first time in my life, I felt genuinely humbled. I thought I knew everything about my family, at least everything I wanted or needed to know, but seeing such living, breathing energy emanating from the representatives, my fictional story collapsed. I re-experienced, first hand, what couldn't even be addressed some forty years before. I finally got to be little, stunned and speechless. As a fifty-plus-year-old adult, I was finally able to let that inner child be the child he had never been, thus releasing the trapped, scared, little boy inside me. It was indescribable. It was wonderful. I just wanted to curl up in a blanket and cuddle. For the first time in years and years, my parents were simply my parents and I was simply their innocent child. The true family order was finally restored inside of me, and I was able to rediscover that order in the outside world, as well. As a result, this experience has allowed me to grow into a more secure adult. That is one of the great lessons of this work. We have to be little first in order to grow up strong. In other words, everything in its proper order. Again, I could actually feel the love I had for those I thought I hated. I could see that the dynamic that my father and I shared came from some other place and some other time and, most likely, from both my parents' family systems. The love I felt for them both burned away the original story from my brain and put another, newer, more vibrant and functional one in its place. It was all for love and nothing else. I had let them hurt me because I loved them so much. Underneath it all, the beatings and violence, although systemic, were signs of the inner strength that I would lovingly hold onto at all cost. I also would suffer for them in any way they needed because my love was so great. Ironically, upon these revelations, I felt less a victim than ever, for I had discovered my power and my say in my own fate. I was able to feel a deep compassion for my mother and father that I had never known before. I realize now that I had loved my father more than I could ever say. I also loved my mother more than I ever knew. I'm sorry that I didn't get to this place sooner but, well, that's life. Of course, they are with me still, even closer to my heart now in death as my breath is their breath manifest in the world until I meet them again in the realm beyond. After all, we are locked into a bigger cycle which we do not really control. Let's enjoy the ride.

HIDDEN RICHES

Ultimately,
it is finding the joy
where there was thought to be none.
It is finding the love
that was hiding beneath the seeds of discontent.
These are all the hidden riches of life,
and when we are willing
to peel off the outer, grimy layer of the story,
we can see the richer truth shine from deep inside,
as LOVE was there all along.
It was just hiding,
waiting until it was safe to come out again,
waiting to see who had the courage to dig deep into the
  unknown
to experience it in all its glory

EXCLUSION

One of the most common and yet most debilitating experiences one can incur within any system is that of feeling excluded. Such a dynamic can take many forms. Someone may simply feel left out of various activities. Some may feel rejected by specific family members. Some may even feel that he or she is being "punished" by the entire group, deemed unfit to be part of their system whether family or not. Sometimes the exclusion is intentional; sometimes it is merely perceived. Regardless, the feeling of being excluded has devastating impacts. Of course, issues of exclusion can even apply to nations, countries and governments. How many wars have been fought over ethnic, cultural or religious differences? Competitiveness and feelings of superiority (and insecurity) can be found wherever life exists, human or otherwise. In this chapter, however, I intend to focus, more or less, on the repercussions of such exclusion within the family system. But, be forewarned. There may be some references to certain political hot potatoes, especially in regard to America's current administrative regime, the institutionalized homophobia it purports and those arrogant, hypocritical, "holier-than-thou" religious factions that further the un-acceptance and exclusion of family members who are different. That said, let us continue.

Every family system has the potential to reject or exclude, and there are numerous ways in which such a dynamic can be exhibited. In some cases, there may have been some traumatic event that generated more pain than the family felt it could endure. As a result, someone or something may have been cast out of the family's consciousness so that the integrity of the overall system would be preserved. Unfortunately, pushing a painful memory away leaves the familial structure less in tact than it would otherwise have been, trauma and all. Not only is such a course of action unfair to those excluded due to their association with the painful event, but it renders a detrimental effect on the entire family system, as well. Furthermore, the stinging memory of whatever transpired does not seem to leave the system but, instead, tends to get repeated down the familial line. Ironically, this is a karmic way of keeping the family system whole and balanced -- and inclusive after all. However, the repetition of familial tragedies is not an ideal construct. The links we share with our ancestors are unquestionably strong. In a sense, their past is a part of us in that they are a part of us, but our future is ours to create. The stories we hear often contain incomplete or sanitized versions of events, and may not accurately represent our family's true nature. Yet, our bonds seem to go even deeper than our DNA. Even those fictionalized stories are conveyed out of love, even though they may unintentionally dishonor an ancestor's memory. Of course, as Hellinger has found, EVERYONE BELONGS. Even those who feel they do not, belong by not belonging. Every single family has a black sheep: a lost uncle, a "bad" girl, gay or lesbian family members, a victim, an alcoholic, a crook -- the list goes on and on. Some judge their family's outcasts as a way to feel superior to their "fallen" relative(s), hiding the fact that they may be an alcoholic, a homosexual, a crook or a murderer themselves. Blaming others is a very convenient way to distract from the skeletons within your own closet. Such ostracizing also creates a sense of family unity for those who agree with the consensus that they are right and the other is wrong. It may be false. It may be self-righteous, but it goes on nonetheless.

As we all know, life has its many twists and turns, and every family deals with them in its own way. Family stories are often constructed so as not to unduly stress or burden future generations. In other words, "If we never mention the crazy uncle, it's as if we never <u>had</u> a crazy uncle." The systemic rule of thumb is often, "Don't scandalize -- Sanitize!" Ironically, the family actually ends up burdening its progeny far more by suppressing information concerning their ancestral history. Still, families continue to agree, on some unspoken level, to paint unfortunate or potentially embarrassing events with a nice, non-threatening whitewash, acceptable to the community at large as well as themselves. As a result, certain relatives and their stories become omitted from the familial storybook, thereby becoming forgotten members of a system where the majority decides the fate of the minority. Yet, every family member needs and deserves respect. In doing his Systemic Constellation work, Hellinger has found, as you'll recall, that future generations will subconsciously pick up on the energy of the excluded one in order to bring him or her back into the fold, as it were. Even if there is a negative association, they will still recognize and include that energy as part of their system. Again, the timetable doesn't matter; family members can identify with relatives who may have been excluded a century before. Many familial splits happen in reaction to some allegedly tragic event befalling a sister, uncle, brother, father, mother -- it matters not who. What is significant, however, is that such divisions often result in exclusion. Curiously, I have observed a great many cases involving sexual abuse that occurred in the late 1800's. While incest, of course, is hardly unique to that time period, still, many families do seem to have sexual skeletons in their late-nineteenth-century closets. Perhaps it may have seemed the answer to fertility problems encountered by a son and his wife. In America's old west, such a situation may have been viewed as catastrophic to the family name. The father may have stepped in to impregnate his daughter-in-law to keep the family line going. While this may, indeed, have been the result, the family order would also be a bit askew, as the grandfather would actually be the father of his grandson, while his son's child would really be his son's younger brother. (See what tangled webs we weave?) That grandchild may have never known who his actual father was; energetically, the exclusion of that knowledge may have impacted his ability to trust or feel secure in his own identity. On a gut level, he might always have felt that some piece of his biological puzzle had been missing. Again, it is imperative that we do not judge anyone or anything when doing a Constellation process. Our intent is to INCLUDE everyone and everything that belongs to the system, thereby restoring the "order of love" and creating harmony where there has been discord. In our example, the proper position of the grandson's biological father had never been filled. Again, this is why re-establishing the correct and true familial order is so important. Once the secret is out, the energy can be released, and the future generations won't have to try to repeat the same mistake for it to be included in the legacy. The family can consciously acknowledge their fertile grandpa and leave it at that.

In other instances, our ancestors may have expressed their repressed sexuality and compensated for their lack of freedom through some good old-fashioned naughtiness. A man, for example, may have had an insatiable libido -- "oversexed," as it used to be called. Unconsciously, he could have been honoring his divorced great grandfather who was a known womanizer and lothario. The old coot may have been, for all intents and purposes, ostracized from the family, an embarrassment to all "descent" folk. Yet, on some systemic, energetic level, his great grandson knew that he had still been part of the system and should not have been excluded for his behavior. As a result, his own sexual appetite reflected that of his infamous predecessor as a karmic way of challenging the family's exclusionary attitude on his great grandfather's behalf. Again, the family system functions best when it includes <u>all</u> its members and their histories. Here's another example. Let's say a woman loves her husband but has been unsuccessful at conceiving a child with him. She may find a lover to give her a child, and yet share the parental duties with her husband even though he isn't the father. This adds another dimension to the family dynamic and sets up another scenario for exclusion -- the type that involves a "missing man." Even if he was merely a sperm donor, he still has to be included as part of the system. A generation or so later, her granddaughter, for example, may have an extra-marital affair and not even know why, yet on some primal level, she is honoring her grandmother and the missing lover to keep the "naughty" myth going within the confines of the family system. Of course, she would also be honoring and including her true biological grandfather, as well. Hellinger has found that even former lovers who yield no genealogical connections with the system often still become bonded to it in some way and should, therefore, be included as part of it. If a man, for example, suddenly dumps his fiancé, then rushes into marriage with the next woman who comes along, the first-born child will often display an affinity toward that missing person -- perhaps the father's true love. Even though she may be excluded from the familial story, her memory still remains within the system and may forge an invisible link with the child. In my own case, I've found that I had a deep identification with my father's first wife, Louise, and that I honestly loved her despite the fact that I was raised by my own mother. Perhaps I was honoring the first family system he had started -- the one that was his at the time of my conception. My mother had her own "I want to be number one" issues and would pit me against my stepsister as a way of releasing her anger at the first wife, the one with whom I continued to identify. From a trans-generational perspective, perhaps Louise had been his first true love. Perhaps he continued to carry her in his heart, even after he had married my mother. Perhaps I subconsciously sensed this and carried her in my own heart as a way of including her in his new family system. It seems we carry so much for others, sometimes it's hard to tell where their issues end and ours begin. Of course, that's precisely how matters of exclusion develop into entanglements.

Another common catalyst for exclusion is death. Often times, grief will manifest in the form of anger, and the dear departed will become a scapegoat or be blamed for his or her own death and for what it has done to the family. Other times, the grief is so overwhelming that it becomes easier to simply avoid it. Some families go so far as to destroy pictures and evidence that their "loved one" had ever existed; therefore, no loss need ever be felt. As you no doubt realize by now, such denial will surly draw future generations to the "fire of incompletion," perhaps even causing them to mimic the same tragedy within the context of their own lives. They may contract the same disease, for example, as a way of keeping the missing one included and remembered. As cited earlier, suicide is another way in which family members often mirror the tragic past. Again, this is why it is so important that we let our ancestors carry their own "stuff," as it were, including the responsibility for their own fates. There are also numerous examples of exclusion involving childbirth. A mother who has a stillborn child may become so distraught that she slips into a state of denial, pretending that it never happened and never speaking of ever being pregnant. Her heart may also turn cold to her husband following such a traumatic event, so not only does the baby become excluded from the system, but the father as well. With this dynamic established, women in that family's future generations may have difficulty getting close to men and may automatically reject them, especially with regard to bearing a child. They could also unknowingly be honoring their female predecessor by simply deciding never to have children at all. Indeed, every stimulus generates a reaction further down the generational line. This applies to abortions, as well. I have seen many cases in which an ancestor has lost a child, perhaps through a miscarriage, and where the granddaughter or great granddaughter then decides to abort her first pregnancy, thereby mirroring a common experience within that family system by re-enacting the loss. One might argue that such a decision could be made completely independent of generational coincidences, and that abortions happen all the time. Perhaps. However, it is in the <u>way</u> that these parallels are revealed in the constellation process that makes the connection relevant. Systemically, let's not forget that the fetus (or child) is the excluded one, and unwanted pregnancies or even issues of infertility may follow as a karmic reminder. Again, Hellinger has observed that everyone and everything is part of the system. If a woman had a miscarriage before having her three children, for instance, she should count that miscarriage as a child within the family, making her a mother of four with the first one "passed on." This inclusiveness completes and honors the entire system within the current generation, thereby giving future ones no subconscious impetus for repeating such a loss. This acknowledgement also creates an extra connection between the surviving family and its member on the "other side," as they say. Think about it. How many of us have missing aunts and uncles -- even sisters or brothers -- that we never knew about? It's almost as if a little dark cloud of the missing one hovers over the family until it is seen and taken in. Only by acknowledging and honoring it can the grief associated with it ever be released. Remember, it's all about completion and inclusion. Hellinger finds that when a couple intentionally decides to abort a child, they will often then kill the marriage as karmic compensation for the life they took. Now, don't get me wrong; I still believe in freedom of choice. The repercussions of our actions, however, are more widespread than we often realize. Unwittingly, we will sacrifice or symbolically lose something else of value in an attempt to balance our internal scale of justice. This is true of other siblings as well -- aligning with death as a tribute of sorts to their lost brother or sister. Again, inclusion is the key.

Of course, there may also be some truly unsavory characters within a family system. Crooks, thieves, murderers -- all are members of families. How do others handle their finances in such a system? Who will copy that behavior in a future generation? If history repeats itself, family history does as well. Always remember that even the most vile of relatives is also included, so it is wise to speak more kindly of them and their problems than to judge what they may have been doing. One never really knows until one has walked in the shoes of another. The worst thing we can do is to say with self-congratulatory pride, "I'm nothing like him!" When it comes to our families, the black sheep isn't always as unique to the flock as we would like to believe. If we truly don't want to be like that shady relative, we must honor and take pride in the whole system, including our connection to that "undesirable" person.

Then there is the matter of injustice within the family system. Perhaps one member of the family steals from another. Perhaps there is jealousy involved, and familial "backstabbing" becomes a toxic energy within the system. Perhaps a great injustice was rendered by a court of law. In any case of this type, just admitting that it has happened is an important first step on the road to resolution. There is also a great release that comes from honoring a person who has suffered an injustice rather than judging the situation or the outcome. The simple act of humbly bowing to them and thanking them for their strength in carrying their fate can release the rest of the system from its negative hold. Furthermore, if an individual should become embroiled in an un-winnable clash of wills with the rest of the family system, simply honoring his or her strength to handle the situation is a respectful way to avoid getting pulled into the fray yourself without excluding or denying anyone his or her place in the family.

Wartime scenarios yield other opportunities for exclusion to occur. Many families have had husbands or sons who never returned from battle due to injury or death. It is very important to include their memory as part of the surviving family so that another sibling does not try to emulate this missing relative by re-enacting his fate. I have seen several cases where a younger brother will enlist in attempt to take his older sibling's place, only to end up following the same tragic path. Other families have had loved ones reported "missing in action," without any further word or resolution. Again, these missing ones are still part of the family system regardless of whether their fates are known or not. This is actually a very good example of how inclusive the system can be, allowing its love to transcend life or death or even the unknown. In other instances, war can set the stage for internal conflicts within the family. A relative might be perceived as a traitor. Perhaps a son was considered a "coward" because he fled the country to avoid having to serve. Perhaps a brother fought for the "wrong side," or a daughter chose to enlist against the wishes of the familial patriarch. Believe me, national politics and political purges can create deep division and cause tremendous turmoil within the "borders" of the family system. During World War II, my father was stationed in France for a bit and, I suspect, may have had an affair with a French girl. Condoms certainly were not in as prevalent a use as they, perhaps, should have been. It is well within the realm of possibility that I may have a "missing" brother or sister in Europe, and I would never even know it. Yet, this is precisely what showed up in a constellation of mine where my whole, immediate family system was represented. Curiously enough, I have been drawn to France many times as a tourist over the years, and love the country nearly as much as my own. It is so amazing how influential the subconscious mind is. It can even take us on a wondrous journey that, ultimately, can help us fill in the missing pages of our family history. Now, that's what I call inclusion!

Another common fuel for exclusionary behavior lies in our religious differences. Since the dawn of time, or at least the dawn of religion, this been one of the quickest and easiest ways to alienate any and all family members who do not interpret the Book (the Torah, the Bible, etc.) in the same way as the others. One "side" always seems to boast the definitive answer when it comes to the practice of faith, often labeling those of other opinions as "sinners," "heretics," or worse. This is also true of countries or nations that preach one religion over any other. Here, at the beginning of the twenty-first century, there seem to be pseudo-systemic battle lines drawn between Christianity and the Islamic Muslim faith. In truth, neither is better and neither is worse, even though the zealots, political and otherwise, will fight to their deaths to prove otherwise. Unfortunately, in trying to exclude and destroy each other's culture, they may well take the whole world with them. Of course, there is actually room for both, although the desire for superiority often overrides such a radical notion. Still, if we truly believed that all faiths were valid -- and treated them as such -- maybe these age-old wars of passion and opposition would finally have an end. We all deserve an equal place at the table of life, regardless of what deity we may or may not worship. People's interpretations of what "God" has said have done more damage in the name of a loving, benevolent creator than He or She could have ever intended. The great irony, of course, is that spirituality, by its very nature, is inclusive. The Spirit, the Soul is what we all share. It is our religions, however, that divide us. Yet, not all religious practices are inherently exclusionary. The important thing to remember is that someone else doesn't have to be wrong in order for you to feel "right." Maybe the Hindu Karmic System practiced in India conveys the most pertinent lesson of all. We do, generationally speaking, reap what we sow. There does seem to be a higher rule of spiritual law, if you will, to which we ultimately must adhere. Although we may try to legislate morality in all kinds of unnatural and hypocritical ways, Divine justice can never be excluded.

Without a doubt, one of the most excluded groups of people in all of human history has been homosexuals, both men and women. Our species has an unfortunate tendency to want to judge others as inferior so that we can feel better about ourselves. Perhaps it's that old "survival of the fittest" thing I mentioned earlier, but no matter how high or how low they were in their social class, some people have always thought, "Well, at least I'm better than those homosexuals!" Such platitudes are still being aggravated and even encouraged by those current minions who try to claim the Bible as a book of fact, rather than a book of faith. They argue that, since it must have been written by God Himself, it could not possibly reflect Man's interpretations of God or His various messages. As you can well imagine, such attitudes of superiority often have resulted in acts of exclusion. I can't even tell you the number of clients I've seen whose parents have practically disowned them because their sexual feelings weren't the same as those of the rest of the family. Often, the majority sees itself as inherently right, castigating the gay, lesbian or bisexual person as inherently wrong. Family members who are trans-gendered, those who have had what is commonly called a "sex change" procedure, often face similar threats of exclusion. Yet, everyone and everything within the family system is a part of that family system and needs to be included as such. As I mentioned at the beginning of this book, that amorphous, undulating mass known as human consciousness knows no boundaries. All of creation thrives on subtle differences, so it makes absolute sense that these differences would be seen in sexuality, as well. Diversity should be celebrated -- perhaps even commended, as these supposedly "queer" folk may actually be saving heterosexuals from extinction through over-breeding! Again, looking at the "big picture," what if homosexuality was a built-in safety mechanism of the Divine life-force to protect the integrity and balance within the finite ecosystem of Earth itself? In other words, if some people weren't gay, we'd <u>really</u> be overpopulated! Statistically, everyone may have a secret gay uncle, sister, cousin, brother, nephew within their own family system. "Shhh… Don't ask; don't tell" is the socially accepted whisper for the American Armed Services, reflecting the less-than-inclusive attitude found in many American families, as well. The pressure to fit in is enormous, and the fear that his or her "secret" may be revealed can be most excruciating for the

102

gay or lesbian family member. Even in this new millennium, acts of unadulterated hatred and cold-blooded murder are reportedly on the rise. Laws have been enacted to condemn such virulent and homophobic actions as "hate crimes," now punishable as such in most states. But why is this attitude, fueled by anger and ignorance, so pervasive in America at this point in time? Are most of these "offended" heterosexual men who are moved to violence actually fearful of their own inner feelings, so they try to squelch them by lashing out at what serves as a reminder of their own discomfort or insecurity? Perhaps they never got to be close to their own fathers, and are now afraid to be close to men because they fear what someone might think of them. I believe there may also be a deeper hatred at work here -- a hatred of the feminine. Again, who could be more inferior, from their bigoted viewpoint, than a woman? A man who acts like one! It is this type of thought process, bolstered by a male-dominated world, that has led so many proud, upstanding, productive citizens to be excluded. Yet, the inner strength that it takes to be different and willing to take a stand may be the very reason certain people are genetically "picked," if you will, to endure this special fate. In other words, even the most excluded ones still belong. They are still, and will always be, a part of every family system, as they have been for thousands of years. Looking once again at the "big picture," is it possible that we pick up, so to speak, where pervious generations left off? Might we/they be identified with another gay person in the family system who could not be open about his or her inclinations? Is today's generation choosing to step forward, stand tall and be counted as a way of honoring their hardships and sacrifices? Might this be how we now include them in our families, rather than continuing to banish them? To all of the above -- YES.

Hellinger has also found an interesting correlation between a parent's former lover -- whom the parent rejected to marry someone else -- and the first-born of the new family system. It seems that child often takes on the feminine or masculine aspects of the father's former flame or mother's previous beau, whichever the case may be. In this way, the jilted fiancé actually becomes included in the new system. I know I've touched on this before, but it bears repeating. Once that true love has taken root in the human heart, the connection travels with us in all we do or create, long after the memory has begun to fade. It seems there is Systemic justice, as well. Again, I loved my father's first wife more than I ever admitted. I even felt "called" to be with her on the day she died, and have very fond memories of her inclusion into our family after the dust of the divorce had settled. Such a situation was rare at this time, but today more and more people seem to be staying on friendlier terms with their exes, perhaps as a consideration to their children, perhaps simply because, in America at least, it seems that everyone has been divorced at least once, myself included. Some families have become very tolerant and have embraced their diversities without judgment or rejection. In my family, there was always talk of my great uncle being "different," although I didn't really understand what was meant by that. As a small child, I liked the guy and always wished I had gotten to know him better. As fate would have it, I ended up being "different," as well, though perhaps not specifically in his memory. Still, maybe there is always someone in every family system who carries this built-in, genetic, human trait. Again, I see it as a Divine safety valve, tempering our population growth and uplifting our species with art, music and literature. There is definitely a purpose and Divine order in all of this, and it is important for us to keep our hearts and minds open. New rationalizations for exclusion also yield new opportunities for inclusion, as well. Families touched by HIV or AIDS may find themselves re-examining their levels of compassion, hopefully strengthening their bonds by continuing to hold their loved ones close. Unfortunately, families who tend to exclude in matters of day-to-day life also tend to exclude in matters of death. A family member's last will and testament has often been used as a final way to exclude certain other family members from the clique. This dance with exclusion, however, always seems to find a willing partner further down the generational line, willing to right the wrong and bring balance and inclusion back into the family system. It all happens like clockwork.

AD NAUSEAM

Guilt crosses all cultural boundaries.
Italians have it. Germans have it. Catholics and Jews think
they own it.
England calls it Monarchy. Muslims call it Martyrdom.
The Chinese call it Tibetan and Tibetans call it Enlightenment.
In pre-Bush America: You were innocent until proven guilty.
In post-Bush America: You stay innocent by changing the
law.
In the new millennium: You're innocent 'til proven celebrity.
If you are a woman, you are guilty 'til proven innocent by man,
for our judicial system is founded on biblical sexism
and hypocrisy.
Guilt is the golden key to most of the world's religions.
It holds the most power and pays the biggest dividend
for absolution.
Sexuality with guilt pays the highest dividend to those
in charge…
unless you work for the church, selling absolution to the
highest bidder.
Meanwhile, they commit unspeakable sins of the flesh
with children and people of the parish.
Maybe they are the only ones who enjoy sex without guilt as
they prey… "Father, I have sinned."
Ad Nauseam.

PERPETRATOR & VICTIM, GUILT & ATONEMENT

*I*f everyone and everything is included in the family system, which it is, this would also apply to its victims and perpetrators, as well as the strange, fateful relationship between them. As I mentioned earlier, when any sort of atrocity is enacted upon any member or members of the family system, the energy of the perpetrator actually becomes part of that system, in that he or she is now part of that family's history. I have seen many clients for whom this has been particularly true. In one instance, a young woman had come to work on her issues concerning feelings of anger and hostility. Her constellation process revealed that her father had been shot and killed under mysterious circumstances when she was a little girl. The perpetrator's aggressive energy was now beginning to manifest in her, and she had even begun to work as a professional wrestler. Though this may have seemed an appropriate outlet for her anger, she still had never expressed it in a manner that would help release her from its hold. This constellation was particularly primal in nature, and her anger was found to be directed at her father and not at his killer. Unconsciously, she was trying to be the strong, aggressive man she felt her father had not been, and she was using the trapped energy from the perpetrator's family system to achieve this goal. Her anger, of course, stemmed from her unexpressed grief, and once it was given voice within the safety of the constellation process, she was able to once again see her father as the kind, capable, loving man he was -- the perfect father for her.

Although profoundly intimate in its systemic revelations and subsequent benefits, this work can also help to provide insight and resolution to dynamics of a much larger scale. Bert Hellinger comments in the prologue to FAREWELL, his masterful book of observations on family constellations with the descendents of victims and perpetrators, that he has repeatedly encountered the effects of the Nazi era on the participants in his courses. Having been confined to a prisoner of war camp himself as a young man, Hellinger found this subject particularly close to his heart. The entanglements felt by those descendents with the fate of the victims and the guilt of the perpetrators have resulted in significant consequences for their present families and have caused tremendous suffering in these later generations. In the constellations set up in these courses, both the victims and the perpetrators were brought back into the family where they could provide support and relief to the suffering of the current family members. The book FAREWELL is the documentation of such encounters, dramatically relating the authentic stories of and by those who were directly affected. The constellations provided the opportunity to pick up the threads of the story at the point where they had been so brutally and inhumanely broken off. Throughout the work, we hear from the survivors as well as the deceased, the guilty as well as the victims, and from the descendents of both sides.

In the constellation process, as you'll recall, all family members, both living and dead, can, in some way, be represented, heard and experienced through the living participants known as representatives. As Hellinger puts it,

"IT IS AS IF AN INTERDEPENDENCE EXISTS BETWEEN THE LIVING AND THE DEAD, WHICH CROSSES THE BOUNDARY OF DEATH." When the deceased are allowed to be represented in this way, it soon becomes clear to the present family members that their own feelings cannot be projected onto them. The dead participate on a different level, where fate overrides our mortal feelings of grief or the need for atonement. Life and death, as well as guilt and innocence, are determined by powers that do not function according to our desires or specifications. Instead, they respond to an order that reaches far beyond the fate of any single individual.

The dead are in harmony with this larger order of things, at least as far as we can see in these constellations, and the descendents of the victims and perpetrators alike find great support and comfort when they are allowed to speak. In grief, people secretly hope to undo what cannot be undone, a desire that permits no end to that which has happened, and continues to burden generation after generation. There is no healing brought about by the descendents sharing the same fate as the dead. More importantly, *"THE DEAD DO NOT ASK FOR SUCH ATONEMENT AND SUFFERING. THE DEAD SEEM TO BE BENIGN TOWARDS THE DESCENDENTS, EVEN THE CHILDREN AND GRANDCHILDREN OF PERPETRATORS, AND DO NOT DEMAND THAT INNOCENT CHILDREN TAKE ON THE GUILT OF THEIR ANCESTORS."*

FAREWELL offers a great contribution toward the process of reconciliation between murders and their victims, and as such, it is also a part of the process of reconciliation between Germans and Jews, as well as Christians and Jews. Indeed, Hellinger offers this book to all who have been affected, either directly or indirectly, by the atrocities of the Third Reich. In my opinion, that includes all of humanity. Let us bow down before the victims and hear as they speak. The perpetrators now also belong to the world of the dead, and Hellinger looks at them together with their victims and makes no attempt to step between them. When it is our turn, we will join them all.

Hellinger goes on to say, "The perpetrator cannot be reconciled with the victims, for example, by asking for forgiveness, even if he or she follows the path of doing something worthy of atonement. This is not because the dead demand revenge. They are on a different level altogether. Revenge does not appease the dead, but rather, honor and grief. In the case of an accident, the attention is drawn to the perpetrator away from the victim's grief. This blocks the grief from being expressed, resulting in the survivor not saying farewell to the dead."

"The dead are reconciled with our pain. When we weep in front of them, it is reconciliation."

"The perpetrator MUST carry the GUILT."

"A perpetrator cannot be exonerated even by doing good things. The guilt remains."

Hellinger also observes:

"Guilt helps us grow."

"Integrating the shadow leads to growth."

"Losing our innocence leads us to growth."

"Solution is achieved when we integrate the excluded into ourselves and our soul."

"Perfection is when all the members of our family have a place in our heart; then we feel free, and no entanglements follow us."

Indeed, life is constantly finding ways to regain its Divine balance. Again, looking at that big, big picture, I honestly believe the tremendous death amassed in Europe during WWII somehow, someway led to a great resurgence of life elsewhere, specifically in America where the "baby boom" helped balance the great death with great life. I may not have been here to write this book -- nor, perhaps, you to read it -- had history not unfolded the way it did. In some strange and ironic way, those attitudes of intolerance and hate may have actually opened a door of love, making it possible for my parents to meet and to make me a recipient of the gift of life. Humbly, I too bow down in honor of the victims and the perpetrators and their respective roles in our modern history. Without them all, life would not be what it is today. Again, L'Chiam!

As a species, we presently find ourselves at another historical crossroads of life and death. The worldwide pandemic of AIDS invites us, once again, to examine our roles, both collectively and individually, as victims and perpetrators. What can this most resent dance with death teach us? Are we all sexual perpetrators or sexual victims? We certainly seem to have the potential to be either -- or both. Perhaps the lesson is that we always have that potential and that we should try to live our lives in neither extreme. Just think of all those un-intentioned perpetrators, forever entangled in the family systems of their sexual partners. The death toll rises every day, and more and more children are born "victims" of their parents' encounter rather than as a pure celebration of it. In that big, Divine balancing act, where and when will the next great emergence of LIFE take place? Perhaps humanity's burgeoning enlightenment is part of that plan.

Nowhere is this constellation work more valuable than in helping us diffuse our entanglements... even those tied to exclusion... and peppered with guilt... and compensated with atonement. In other words, no matter how screwed up your life may feel, it really can regain its wonderful order. The constellation process allows us an energetic window into the past like no other modality to date. We only need to have the courage and willingness to face those unknown dynamics that affect our lives in negative ways for the seeds of profound change to be fertilized and made ready to sprout into new awareness. When we allow the trapped energies to move from the exclusionary past into the inclusive present, the truth can be shown, the entanglements unraveled, the guilt admitted and no atonement will be deemed necessary. It all will rest in peace with the real victims and the real perpetrators. When we at last become free of our ancestral chains, we need only offer a humble "thank you" to all concerned and a humble bow to the drama that is life. Being able to honor and respect the events in our pre-history as necessary steps leading to the personal gift of our creation is truly the greatest reward we could offer -- or receive. Others suffered so that we could live and, with any luck, enjoy this glorious life with all its beauty and splendor, free of any binds that tie us to a situation that no longer exists. This is how we can truly honor those who came before us -- by replacing their suffering with joy and humble gratitude, that we sincerely appreciate all of the gifts that we have been given.

To life!

GIVE

Give Breath

To the memory of those whose bodies have disappeared from the earth. Speak of them kindly, as they may be near enough to listen.

Give Heart

To all the thoughts and feelings that sometimes refuse to leave even when their emotional charge is gone. Love them as you do life.

Give Ears

To the weight of all words spoken and unspoken whether they be dreams expressed or promises broken. Listen intently...

Give Hope

To the dead, as they live on in our hearts with the memories we gather before we depart. To honor the dead, this is the start.

Give Love

To any and all as much as you can, as life is too short for the human lifespan. There is nothing better to say than I love you and hope you're OK.

Give Honor

To those who raised you when you were so small, for it is these parents who started it all. Remember to honor them when you've grown tall.

Give Respect

To your elders -- never let it refrain, as the baggage you will inherit will cause you great pain -- because, after all, we're really the same.

Give Peace

To those who've passed, and please let them go. They've moved up a notch to go with Divine flow. You'll be with them again, sooner than you know.

Give everything you can; there is nothing you will lose.
You have everything to gain from what you hear, say and do.

THE HOLOGRAPHIC PRISM

O f all the amazing aspects of Bert Hellinger's work, this well may be the most difficult to convey, yet it is at the very heart of how the process is able to achieve its profound results. The inherently spiritual implications of his discoveries seem to indicate that every human being, as a result of his or her very creation, embodies all that was ever known or experienced within this incredible human journey of ours. Within our genetic structure, beneath our conscious perceptions, lies an energetic field of awareness that reacts to life's various stimuli, triggering those natural and inherent responses programmed into us before our birth. We're often too focused on our senses of taste, touch, smell, hearing and sight that we miss those other natural senses we possess within the field of our own life force. (I know this gets a little esoteric, but stay with me here.) These subtle, ever-present energies offer us support and guidance, just as they did for our ancestors... and their ancestors... and theirs -- as far back as time itself. Our very life force seems to spring eternal from the realms of invisible consciousness, feeding the subtle energy contained within our body, mind and soul. These unseen forces seem to operate within the realm of our daily existence while simultaneously never losing their connection to the forces and energies that connect all living things together as one. These forces seem to possess a holographic nature containing the Spirit of Life from whence we all came. The "realists" who think that what you see is all that you get may be in for a rude awakening. The unseen forces of creation operate within you and without you, and they are the very source of your existence. Seeing their hidden dynamics in operation beneath the surface will truly leave you awestruck, as it continues to do for me. From a systemic standpoint, each individual is endowed with all the collective information of the family's experiential history, both conscious and otherwise, as well as the emotional context of the events that caused those other generations to react as they did. This may be easier to comprehend with regard to the animal kingdom. Many species instinctually know where and what to eat as they crawl or swim out of the womb or waddle to the water after hatching on land. They also seem to instinctually know who their natural predators are, as well as knowing how to allude such enemies. Every species seems to be consciously "hardwired" for survival prior to any direct experience, perhaps even prior to its physical incarnation. Of course, isn't that what "instinct" is all about? Humankind also has its connections to nature's energetic, instinctual realms. Whether we are conscious of it or not, our invisible hardwiring exists. Any altered state or non-ordinary conscious experience will demonstrate the untapped capability of the human mind. Our individual, spiritual consciousness is very much like a prism reflecting shimmering aspects of itself back to its creator. Nowhere is this more evident than from child to his or her parents. To put it poetically, it's as if the light of love between the two parents creates a new and unique being to reflect the light of that love back to them. This smiling baby is surely the face of God smiling back on its creator with glowing and unconditional love and a giggle, as if to say, "I get all of this and fun too!" Indeed, we do. Of course, the parents are also witnessing something bigger than themselves contained within their offspring. They are also looking at <u>their</u> creator -- the one who created their new role as parents. They are also looking at a pure, unadulterated incarnation of the great life force itself.

Again, Hellinger finds that the "reaching out" movement of a child to a parent, especially the mother, is perhaps the single most important act of bonding (or attempt at bonding) that we will ever experience in this lifetime. If the reach is not reciprocated or if this warm, nurturing, comfortable bond is broken, stressed or tampered with in any way, it is almost guaranteed that a lifetime of insecurities or mistrust will follow. You can imagine the trans-generational implications with regard to matters of adoption. As loved and wanted and nurtured as a child may be by the adoptive family, he still carries an inherent consciousness of his biological family system within his genetic makeup. He is, therefore, still subject to the hidden forces at work within his birth family's "knowing field." It seems as if, along with a body, we inherit the collective unconsciousness of our entire biological family system even without any concrete knowledge of our biological heritage. It is as though two disconnected realities must coexist simultaneously within the framework of each adopted child, much like a planet orbiting within a larger star system containing two separate suns -- two different gravitational pulls. Such binary systems can often be challenging to navigate. I have heard numerous cases of adults who felt "split" inside, always feeling conflicted or divided, always sensing someone or something was missing, only to discover they had been adopted into a different biological family. Again, as loving and supportive as those parents may have been, our physiological connection to our genetic family system will not allow itself to be forgotten. One particular constellation I recall involved a client's adopted daughter who had begun exhibiting quite a bit of anger toward both of her adoptive parents during her pubescence. It became obvious during the process that the girl felt a direct, emotional connection to the mother of her biological father (hence, her biological grandmother). Her father had been an unwanted child himself, and had never dealt with his feelings of abandonment toward his birth mother. When he became a father himself, he then put his own daughter up for adoption -- the daughter who was now an adolescent. The anger she was expressing was her biological grandmother's, who had projected the unresolved issues from her own youth onto her son during his uncertainty about "keeping" his daughter. This systemic anger, present in the biological side of the child, was now being projected onto the adoptive family, even though she had been adopted by them the moment she was born. Although she had never interacted with or, at that time, even known her genetic family system, she had "inherited" these feelings, so to speak, and was now acting them out on her current family situation. Despite her upbringing by the adoptive parents, she still carried the "systemic disposition," if you will, to give a future child of hers up for adoption as well, thereby honoring her biological family's pattern of behavior. Once the anger was released through the representative during the constellation process, the daughter's frustration and anger subsided within two days, even though she herself hadn't been physically present while the work was being done. As she matures into adulthood, many other issues are likely to arise as other facets of her biological family's system reveal themselves. Someday she may even get the opportunity to meet her birth mother or biological father, helping her to further understand all of the common traits she shares with these total strangers who created her. Not only will this be a big "ah, ha" moment for the daughter but for her long lost mother or father, as well. In this particular case, the biological grandmother's legacy was still being reflected through that holographic, generational prism evidenced in her granddaughter's physical existence. After the constellation was complete, there was a great sense of peace within the adoptive mother's psyche. Frankly, she was relieved that her adopted daughter's anger wasn't really about her. Indeed, even with no physical contact or relationship established beyond the genetics involved in our creation, we still inherit an energetic, ancestral field of information that is as much a part of who we are as our bodies themselves.

One can never predict what the results of the released dynamics will be or when and how they will later manifest within the client's life. We are accessing a dimension that has been unobserved or unintentionally closed prior to the process. Essentially, we are clearing a pathway for something new to transpire rather than seeing a repetition of the "same old, same old" generational pattern. Some shifts, either internal or external, happen quickly. Others move more slowly and take root deep below the observable surface. The emphasis is on helping the person working to be more open to the unknown forces that direct the process to the best resolution possible. Fate may alter its course around the issue or destiny may transform and move it into a new and unexpected direction. Always remember, "*Within the energy of the problem lies the seed of the resolution.*" Everything we experience contains a gift; it is in the delicate unwrapping that it will reveal all of its surprises. The systemic energy of truth will shine its light on those places that once had seemed so dark. Of course, the "light" was there all along; we just couldn't see where it was hiding. The constellation process allows us a window into the inner workings of those hidden dynamics that fuel the life force's subtle subconscious contained within every one of us, every day of our life -- and beyond. Where my theory of a "holographic prism" comes into play is in our interconnection to those previous generations who are no longer alive at the time the work is being done. I have witnessed what I call "the wisdom of the dead" on many occasions, experiencing unbelievable amounts of stimuli relayed through my body in the form of thoughts or sensations. The energy and the information come from within the "knowing field" of every person's genetic history, and it is embodied within each and every individual. Often, the person representing an issue or family member may have a very similar family dynamic within his or her own system, resulting in healing effects for both the client and the representative simultaneously. The frequent connection to aspects of another's familial field leads me to this "holographic" way of looking at the prismatic effects seen in Hellinger's Trans-Generational process. In other words, the field will direct the person working to choose someone with the same issue to be a representative, thereby allowing both participants' journey into the unknown to be a fulfilling and, ultimately, a healing one. This systemic energy may also point to a negative identification or unseen entanglement with an event or relative unknown to the family member working on his or her own, seemingly unconnected issue. It is often surprising where the "knowing field" takes us, and we must always let it remain in charge. Eventually, it will reveal where it or the appropriate family members "got stuck," as it were, and what resolution may be possible. Whatever the outcome, we must be able to recognize the present moment as containing all the possibilities of life, and that all is accessible to those who have the courage to experience it. This work offers, with love, a different way of looking at that hidden pain, frozen in time and carried in our subconscious. Often, a client may not initially have the slightest idea where the energetic story emerged from, yet he or she will feel the depth of its accuracy. Remember, if we can alter our perception of the past, we can create a different probability for the future -- which is, generally, why a client comes to this work in the first place. Usually, something in his or her life is not working or he/she needs some help to feel more fulfilled. Perhaps they keep hitting the same roadblock and are seeking to change some dysfunctional pattern. Some may resist, as they are loyal to their familiar, familial baggage. Perhaps they are entangled with the negative energy of a missing or excluded relative. Perhaps they feel it is their job to carry the pain (whatever that might mean) for the rest of the family. Such systemic bonds are stronger than any link of trust they may have with a facilitator, and such loyalty must be respected. What this work provides, therefore, are the alternative ways in which we can remain connected and true to our family systems without necessarily following the same fate. This can be especially relevant where disease is concerned. Understandably, we may not want a negative entanglement with a relative who suffered or died from cancer or another terminal disease. There are many other ways to show or demonstrate loyalty without repeating the same tragic pattern. We can acknowledge their fate as theirs and only theirs. We can remain connected to them by remembering them and keeping them included in the family system. What's more, we can work to release the core grief that may have been a contributing cause of disease in the first place. By honoring those who suffered in a direct and forthright manner, we open ourselves to their blessing and guidance until it is our turn to join them. Those unresolved issues of our family's past that we tend to carry out of love or guilt have an invisible tension to them. This lack of harmony inhibits the vitality of the life force rather than strengthening it. When we acknowledge and release the hidden dynamic of the issue within the context of this work, we can feel a tension-free peace sweep through the room as though a static charge of energy was neutralized through the resolution attained during the process. This release and subsequent healing also extends out to the actual family members involved in the issue whether they are present or not. This holographic effect of the process is what allows the representatives, through "quantum osmosis," if you will, to resolve the issue on behalf of its "real" owner. Therefore, if need be, the work can be done by one family member (the client) unbeknownst to the rest of his or her family. It seems that each individual, although part of a family system, is also a self-contained and conscious piece of a still bigger system which also allows access to all its other pieces. Each individual member, therefore, is actually at the systemic center of his or her own universe, as well as the center of the bigger system. (I know, I know. It's a bit esoteric, but we're dealing with the larger field of life here.) We all live in a sea of infinite possibilities, rife with unimaginable outcomes. When we change one piece of the puzzle, all the others are affected accordingly. Each choice we make in the present, although influenced by those of the past, propels life forward in search of an answer or a missing puzzle piece, to find a good solution or to release any negative ties that bind. By releasing our hold on the past, we allow it to release its hold on us. This movement toward wholeness may well be the driving force of life itself. Remember, it is all about an undulating consciousness seeking union, completion and fulfillment. It all exists to tell the story of our journey of discovery, to again become one with all living things -- and those no longer living, as well.

Again, one of the most exciting aspects of this work is that we can actually alter the systemic perceptions of anyone's "holographic field" and extended family system. This process helps us reflect with wonder and awe on the true, positive meaning of life itself. Similar to our consciousness, we are all seeking a deep sense of fulfillment, and whether it is attained through a positive or a negative prism is of little concern to us. Perhaps we knew of this drama and its consequences before we ever arrived for our current incarnation. As the saying goes, "We may have come to re-experience how we got to where we knew that we were going to end up all along!" Indeed, I sometimes feel like an archeologist, digging into my past to witness in the present how I got to the future from whence I came. And what could be more "holographic" than that?

TRANSFORMATION

"So why are we exploring all of this in the first place?" -- you may ask. Simply put, it's so we can become more functional adults and have a fuller, more productive, healthy, loving existence throughout our lives. With the insight provided by this work, we can be open to and truly present with the wonder of all creation that is ours during our span of time here on Earth. This living experience is a divine drama, and we can learn from and share all of life's ups and downs, joys and sorrows as we explore this Earth and complete our destiny within this realm of duality, as it were. One of the biggest achievements I find with this work is that we are finally able to take our rightful place in our family, in life, within ourselves. It is finally time to relinquish the patterns that don't serve us and take charge of every aspect of this incarnation, improving what we can, accepting what we cannot. This is what adults do. We have a choice, regardless of our perceived loyalties or duties within the family system. We may carry the grief and depression only to be further victimized by some incurable disease. Perhaps fate is just fate, and nothing can be done to alter it. Yet, one can never know with certainty what one's fate is going to entail. Perhaps it is our destiny to die trying to change it. There is also the potential, given the right set of discoveries and actions, that another fate may welcome those who dared to dream the impossible. Life is, after all, a cosmic crapshoot, and we are the dice, our Earth is the table, and God is the big player. Maybe that is who we are all in service to in the first place. I'm sure He/She will be anxious to see how we interpreted our experience in this dimension of the physical and what spiritual lessons we learned from it all. When we come from a place of wholeness, we really can do no wrong. Only to learn what all we can from whatever we have done. As I've mentioned, it was through my initial exposure to this work that I was finally able to separate myself from the label of "victim" I gave myself as a child in a world full of hostile giants. It's amazing how owning our own stuff, as it were, and embracing a few, simple truths can actually give us the strength to release what isn't serving us, no matter how comfortable or familiar it may be.

A few years ago, a dear friend's son was being particularly "bratty" -- really acting out all over the place. That very evening, I called my own mother and apologized for having been such a big brat and for my part in encouraging her to beat me. She was taken aback, to say the least, saying, "I never thought I'd live to see the day where YOU admitted you did something wrong!" Although, at first, she tried to make light of it, she had heard the sincerity in my voice, and continued, "I'm sorry for how I reacted. Always know I loved you anyway because you were my first son." This was actually my first big step into true adulthood. I had agreed to carry the weight of my own fate and, thus, allowed her to carry hers. Although we were equals in that sense, I was still letting her be my mother and still respecting her as the adult she was. It marked a pivotal change in our relationship. For the first time in my life, I stopped whining, "She hit me and abused me." By admitting the truth that I had encouraged it as much as she had, I leveled the playing field, so to speak, and finally saw us as both simply human. We so often remain victims as adults because we subconsciously think our parents aren't strong enough to carry the weight of their actions. They are. By doing so, they regain their dignity and self-respect. By continuing to play the "victim," we continue to carry the weight, thus denying them their responsibility and their chance at redemption, which, consequently, denies us our own. This is how Bert Hellinger's discoveries can truly help. His modality allows us to take our place, know our place, accept how it all happened and, above all, see how we **consent** to it. This is what adulthood means. The past may not be undone, but its ramifications can be transformed to create a brighter future. It is our perception that has to change, and everything else will follow. We can release the generational hold of the past by embracing it with love and honor, and by believing that it simply was as it had to be. Now, they can carry their part and we can carry ours. Again, our parents will always be our parents, and we will always be their child, just as they will always be our grandparents' children. We are always "small" in our original family system, even after we start one of our own. This is all part and parcel, if you will, of belonging to a family. Ironically, it was seeing my dear friend's child acting like a mini-me that inspired my journey into adulthood. Special thanks to Isaac for reminding me of what I was yet to become. I know that someday I'll be reaching back to the part of him that was me to return the favor. Our two family systems may seem completely dissimilar, and we are not blood related at all; still, higher forces have intertwined our lives forever, as they have for others. In fact, many people find the motivation for their most profound changes in those to whom they seem least connected. Perhaps it is the freedom we feel from a family system other than our own -- freedom from the patterns, freedom from restrictions, freedom to explore and discover who we might really be. Such inter-systemic entwining may also be part of our fate. They are certainly divinely orchestrated by those bigger forces at work, providing mystery and occasional chaos, but also part of life's intelligent, grand design found in every level of existence -- from protozoa to people.

The beauty of Hellinger's observations is that they provide a "way out" of our old patterns by allowing us to see our problems with fresh eyes, so to speak. Again, his Constellation process allows us a window into the inner workings of life's spiritual checks and balances, helping us to see the inherent order of things and understand why they are as they are. It is truly a glorious opportunity to glimpse the invisible and unknown forces that shape the elements of our daily lives. We get to see, hear, feel and fully perceive that positive charge where once there was only a negative perception. The results are as difficult to describe as the work itself, yet they are easy to feel and understand once experienced in context. This process gives us the chance to witness and honor the suffering of those who came before us and to truly feel compassion for a fate very much worse than our own. It is important to do so, of course, so that we can separate ourselves from it. We must be able and willing to bow down with respect to them, for they were our creators, and we must remain humbled by them. Again, when we allow ourselves to be small, we give ourselves room to grow. Our ego mind tells us we are in control; but to truly be, we must be willing to relinquish it to certain, greater forces. This is one of the Divine paradoxes of our dualistic universe. We all have the same propensity to suffer, yet we also share the same propensity for joy. We are all unique individuals, yet we are all the same. Only the stories of how we came to be are different. We are all one under the sun, no one better, no one worse -- just equal. The more I experience this modality's wonderful peak into the systemic family dynamics of the human race, the more this pearl of wisdom regarding equality seems to prevail. Positive change starts from within. When we open our hearts to the unknown, a new perception of the "truth" can enter. Perhaps what we have perceived as negative has merely been an illusion filtered through unopened eyes of those who came before. Perhaps we carried their burdens because we thought we were supposed to in order to belong. Truth is, we belong anyway. We don't have to do anything to belong. We don't have to prove anything to belong. We don't have to pay any price to belong. We may still want to, but that is our choice; therefore, we can choose not to. I honestly believe that this is our ancestors' wish for us -- to be able to simply enjoy the wonders of life unencumbered, as perhaps they could not. They do not want or need us to carry their baggage for them. This, again, speaks to the amazing "quantum" property of this Constellation work. By altering our legacy, we alter theirs. Perhaps we can be the ones who finally bring a sense of inner peace back to our family system. Perhaps, when we can truly see this world as the beautiful, loving, perfect place that it is, those who came before us will see it through our eyes, as well. Perhaps they will then truly rest in peace, knowing that we finally "get it." Loving life and living life in its entirety is where enlightenment begins. Welcome to love. Welcome to life. Welcome to a future you might never have thought possible.

For everything in our lives to transform, only one thing has to -- our perception. This work affords us that opportunity.

"REFLECTION"

I thought you were my enemy
I'M SORRY
I saw you as greedy
AND IT WAS ME NEEDING VALIDATION
I saw you as angry and cold
IT WAS MY INABILITY TO SPEAK UP WARMLY
I couldn't see you
BECAUSE I WAS BLIND
Now I see you
IT WAS ME BEING UNKIND
I was just growing
I HOPE YOU DON'T MIND
You were reflecting me
ASPECTS I COULDN'T SEE
I was reflecting you
SOMETHING WE BOTH NEVER KNEW
When we fight it's to always be "RIGHT"
WE WERE BOTH RIGHT ALL ALONG
And couldn't harmonize our song
BECAUSE MAYBE "we" BOTH FEEL WE DIDN'T
BELONG
with or to each other
NOW I KNOW THAT THIS ISN'T SO
We both were too strong to get along
NOW WITH THIS KNOWLEDGE WE BOTH CAN
BE STRONG
by thanking each other all life long.

THE RELEASING POWER OF "THANK YOU"

*F*or some odd reason, people often look to the most complicated means for resolving their interpersonal dilemmas. Perhaps our conflicts become so familiar, so comfortable, if you will, that we really can't imagine them being resolved at all. We seem to get so caught up in proving that we are right, stubbornly waiting for the other person to change or do something different, that we forget that we can do something different ourselves. We forget that some of the simplest gestures have the power to take the ego-driven wind right out of people's self-righteous sails. Believe it or not, I find that thanking -- yes, <u>thanking</u> -- is one of the most powerful and humbling things that we could ever do to release ourselves from any negative ties that bind us to anyone or anything. Yes, it seems like the last thing we would ever think to do to or for a perceived enemy. It's also the last thing we would ever consider doing with regard to a parent whom we believe did something wrong or made some mistakes in that less-than-perfect upbringing of ours. Yet, this is the quickest and simplest way of disengaging from that dysfunctional path of cynicism so well traveled in American society today. Why, you may ask, is thanking the person we think least deserves it such a good thing to do? Because doing so inherently changes the dynamic between the estranged parties. Of course, sometimes we don't so much want the problem to be resolved as we do our "terms" to be met. When both sides feel this way, which, being human, they often do, the road to resolution reaches an impasse, and the energy of the conflict gets stuck in the system(s) of those involved. Therefore, as a way of helping to defuse such future entanglements, it is really rather wise to show a simple sign of respect, even if we cannot comprehend why the recipient is deserving of it. We often have a cesspool of rationalizations churning as to why we shouldn't acknowledge this person in a positive light. "She used to beat me." "He was never there for me." Do it anyway. Let me repeat that. **Do it anyway** -- if for no other reason than as an experiment in trusting what you may not understand, and as a way of surrendering to the unknown. To keep doing things as you always have and yet to expect different results is not only unrealistic, it's a tad delusional. If something has to change, let the change start with you. To make it easier, think of it as thanking them for their candor in showing you who they really are. That way, you won't have to give up your negative judgments of them all at once. We humans seem to hold onto our negativity as if it were a prized possession. Still, we have the capability of letting it go, and it's never too late to do so. Even if the person we feel anger toward is no longer living, we can still thank them for sharing who they really were with us. Such knowledge yields clarity, and for that, at least, we can be grateful. Of course, there's another consideration. That very person we seem to despise might just be a mirror that we refuse to face. By continuing to carry resentment, we continue to carry the ugly reflection of our perceived nemesis within us, thereby still allowing him or her to have power over us. The result, of course, is that we still feel like victims. This is not a badge of honor, however, and we should be willing to relinquish our self-imposed claim to the title. Perhaps we are angry with ourselves for trusting this person enough to become hurt by them. Perhaps our anger is merely spilling over onto him or her because we want to be able to trust again but secretly fear that we will not. What if we acknowledged our vulnerability and willingness to love, even though we may have been hurt or disappointed by our presumed perpetrator? In reality by thanking this person, we are acknowledging our part in the drama. By doing so, we regain our power. Furthermore, we release ourselves, as well as any possible progeny, from the energetic grip of the entanglement. To walk around with a poisoned heart is hardly a privilege, and it certainly isn't worth the price of never again trusting or loving the rest of the human race. It is even possible to thank yourself for stopping the pattern of endlessly searching for answers as to how or why this happened to you in the first place. Maybe your perceived enemy doesn't warrant your wrath after all. We can't really change another person, but we can change our perception by showing gratitude for whatever lessons we've learned from our dealings with this allegedly "bad" person. When we feel venomously toward someone else, we poison ourselves. In this simple act of thanking, we are able to bypass the ego and give our hearts free reign to soar beyond the petty dramas we tend to take so seriously. Maybe the anger we project onto the world is a manifestation of our ego not willing to relinquish its control over our objectivity. This may be where the real battle lies.

The healing power of resolution and reconciliation has an incredible effect on every aspect of our body, mind and soul. Finding love and appreciation releases us from what we do not understand and strengthens us, as well as the person onto whom we may have projected our angst. The truth is often more subjective than we realize. If we can examine our internal landscape and acknowledge those "buttons" that were in place long before the external stimuli even came along, we can actually begin to take responsibility for our reactions instead of blaming outside forces for them. Perhaps this is part of the path to enlightenment. It surely is a part of the path to adulthood. Of course, we are all hardwired for the same "fight or flight" response, and expect it to yield a satisfactory solution to the problem at hand. Often, however, it doesn't. My exposure to Hellinger's work has afforded me more space inside myself, so to speak, allowing me room to pull back, observe what buttons of mine were pushed and to realize that I have the choice not to react, knowing what my issues are and taking into consideration what theirs may be. Within this sense of space and inner peace, without having to utter a single word, I thank the person for reminding me of an issue I still may not have fully resolved. That button may still be there, but I know that if someone pushes it, it's only because I have allowed them to do so. I'm still human, just one who's no longer a victim.

In doing Primal Constellation work, the issues we should first seek to resolve are those we have with other members of our family. If we can make progress there, dealing with matters of social interchange should be a piece of cake. In American culture, we often tend to blame fathers for not being present, despite their archetypal role as breadwinner -- working to provide the money for food, shelter and protection for himself, his wife and the rest of his family. Of course, many mothers also work and earn a paycheck for their families. However, there still exists a substantial discrepancy with regard to our attitudes concerning these two familial roles. By labeling fathers as "absent" or not caring as much as the mother, we tend to foster a cultural disregard for the male. Again, if we can get to a place of thanking this man for all he did, acknowledging that he too may have sacrificed greatly for the wellbeing of his brood, then we can move from a place of judgment (which weakens us) to a place of honor and respect (which strengthens us). Such a change in attitude not only helps to create a sense of inner peace but a sense of familial harmony as well. This is applicable regardless of individual circumstance. In other words, even if you never knew your father at all, even if he simply impregnated your mother and left, he still deserves to be thanked. Remember, you would never have even been here, never would have known this experience called life without his "contribution." Of course, this is precisely where matters of parental loyalty come into play. Even though 50% of who that child is would have come from such a father, an abandoned mother might well harbor ill feelings toward him and unconsciously, or even intentionally, may teach the offspring to "side" with her against him. She was, after all, left holding the bundle, as it were. Out of love, the systemic message, "You can't trust men" will likely be embraced by the child, and he or she may well have difficulty with intimacy later in life. If a girl, she may find herself drawn to men who will prove the familial caveat correct. If a boy, he may find himself living up to the cliché as well, thereby showing his connection to the father he had rejected as an obedient son. If the child, now grown, can somehow reconcile with his missing parent, even in the form of a surrogate representing him, the strength derived from such a re-bonding with this masculine force will change every aspect of the person's life. In effect, when we thank and honor both of our parents, we make ourselves whole. Including the excluded has a very powerful and strengthening effect. Hellinger finds that if we cannot honor our creators, we are doomed to grind an axe of self-contempt, which weakens us immeasurably. Part of maturity, a big part, is learning how to love life for what it is, rather than resenting it for not being what it "should" have been. The power of acceptance is a positive force, and it can help us to grow whenever and wherever we choose to begin the maturation process. Again, a simple "thank you" is a great place to start. Thank your parents for having you, then let your gratitude extend to others within your family system. Thank your siblings, aunts, uncles, grandparents and the rest for their part in making your unique family all that it is. That pyramid of support behind you will be all the more solid when you, the capstone of your generation, become the cornerstone for those who come after you. Ultimately, your gratitude will extend beyond the sphere of your personal acquaintances to include all of humanity -- indeed, all living things. It really is all about love, strength and acknowledging what is. When we are willing to take our generational place and to be small, gracious and humble, then and only then can we enter into a happy, harmonious and healthy adulthood.

BOW DOWN

Bow down to all those that came before us as they remain alive at your innermost core, seeing the world through your eyes.

Bow down to the suffering and strife that your ancestors endured surviving the conditions that led to your life.

Bow down to all the pain that life may have caused, for you are the JOY of their toil and labor that can't be ignored.

Bow down yet again to your very own parents, even if their gifts to you were never apparent.

Bow down to the mysteries of life that fail to make sense; it's God's way of showing there's always a chance.

Bow down to it all, no matter what you think. If you do not stop to do this, your life could be gone in a blink.

To *bow down* is a humble act of honoring those who came before. If you can't *bow down* to your creator, then what in your life means more?

Bow Down...

EPILOGUE

*T*hroughout this book, I have attempted to communicate the incommunicable. Life's profoundness lies in what we experience, not what we are told. Still I believe the human species is at the dawn of a new age -- a personal and collective awakening to the Divine interconnection of all things. As science discovers more about the quantum nature of the universe, we can apply this knowledge to our own internal processes -- the Quantum Mechanics of the Human Spirit, if you will. Being able to observe the ways in which this information connects us to the outer realms of the life force or even to the realm of the "dead" is one of the most groundbreaking discoveries of our time.

Congratulations to Bert Hellinger for being such a daring pioneer in his understanding of human consciousness and its interaction with our ancestral energies and the primal, multidimensional forces that affect us all on a daily basis. This universe we inhabit is a magnificent laboratory of the Creator, and everything fits together in a great, cosmic tapestry of organized chaos and intelligence. Every piece balances the rest, exemplifying the universal harmony found within all things, living or dead.

Albert Einstein searched his whole life for ways to mathematically prove what was in his Grand Unified Theory (his GUT). I believe the work of Bert Hellinger and his Constellation process has come very close to solving -- or at least rendering accessible -- how we can experience the space/ time continuum with immediate, truthful and emotionally pertinent results. Not only can we see, hear and feel those dynamics hidden within the Tree of Life, we, as its leaves, can explore the skinny branches of our own budding awareness. Hellinger has tapped into something pretty amazing here, and, in my opinion, it's not a moment too soon. The old paradigm of "winners" and "losers" is coming to an end; humanity is in the process of uniting into an enlightened state of "oneness" -- rather, an awareness of our oneness. As Tom Joad observes in *The Grapes of Wrath*, "Maybe... a fella ain't got a soul of his own, just a little piece of a big soul -- the one big soul that belongs to everybody." It is precisely this prospect that makes Hellinger's wonderful and profound work possible. Perhaps this realization of our "oneness" is part of what Enlightenment is all about. But attaining Enlightenment isn't about having learned something; it's about having become that something -- having become aware of who we are, of who we **all** are, and it's about living in that state of knowledge. It's an ambition both lofty and primal, and though Hellinger himself may modestly deny it, I believe he and the Trans-Generational process he has developed could well be at the forefront of this evolution of awareness.

Life is good, and it is all connected by one grand, unifying substance -- the eternal energy of unconditional love. May we all have the opportunity within our lifetime on Earth to explore the field of unlimited possibility while we live and inhabit the field of pure potentiality.

Namaste, *Gary*

TRANS-GENERATIONAL SYSTEMIC CONSTELLATION CONTACT INFORMATION AND RESOURCES

Gary Stuart's website is
www.TransGenerationalGroup.com
I have numerous links to other facilitators in the U.S.
My first book **God says, HEAL!**
and my second book (a novel)
2004: Nature of the Beast by Big Brother
are both available at www.Amazon.com

Bert Hellinger's website is **www.Hellinger.com**

My teacher **Heinz Stark's** website is
www.StarkInstitute.com

Most of Bert's books are available on **www.AMAZON.com**
And also **www.ZeigTucker.com** with video series as well
His recommended readings to date are.
Loves Hidden Symmetry
Acknowledging What Is
Supporting Love
On Life and Other Paradoxes
Love's Own Truths

Insights: Lectures and Stories

Peace begins in the Soul

Farewell: Family Constellations with Victims and Perpetrators

To the Heart of the Matter: Brief Therapies

Touching Love: Bert Hellinger at Work with Family Systems

Touching Love, Volume 2: A Teaching Seminar

Many video series of live workshops filmed Globally during various workshops also available at Zeig, Tucker & Theisen Inc.

A Yearly Magazine published out of England **The Knowing Field** at **www.SystemicSolutions.co.uk**

Other highly recommended readings:

The Healing of Individuals, Families & Nations by John Payne

"The Field" by Lynne McTaggart

You're One of Us! By Marianne Franke-Gricksch

Images of the Soul: The workings of the Soul in Shamanic Rituals and Family Constellations by Daan van Kampenhout

The River Never Looks Back and **In the Minds Eye**: Family Constellations in Individual Therapy and Counselling both by Ursula Franke

Rachel Weeping for Her Children:
Family Constellations in Israel

The Art and Practice of Family Constellations Leading Family Constellations as Developed by Bert Hellinger written by Bertold Ulsamer

Other great authors:

The Seth Material by Jane Roberts (any & all books)
Molecules of Emotion by Candace Pert
The Eagles Quest by Fred Alan Wolf (any and all books)
Books human sexuality and sexual diversity by Simon LeVay

ORGANIZATIONS Exploring Consciousness:

An American Organization to expand conscious thought.
The Institute of Noetic Sciences website **www.noetic.org**

The Society for Scientific Exploration the conscious pulse of
the planet and collective human reactions to event stimuli.
www.ScientificExploration.org

Last but not least, my personal evolution of studying many
modalities for the past 30 some years and being a facilitator
has led me to a new way to describe the work I currently do
in Los Angeles and elsewhere -- the Primal Constellation
Experience.

Printed in the United States
89469LV00003B/244-267/A

9 781420 870930